From Here to
Retirement

Planning NOW
for the Rest of Your Life

From Here to
Retirement

Paul
Fremont
Brown

WORD BOOKS
PUBLISHER
WACO, TEXAS

A DIVISION OF
WORD, INCORPORATED

FROM HERE TO RETIREMENT

Unless otherwise indicated, Scripture quotations are from The Holy Bible, New International Version (NIV). Copyright © 1973, 1978, 1984 International Bible Society. Used by permission of Zondervan Bible Publishers.

Library of Congress Cataloging-in-Publication Data

Brown, Paul Fremont, 1921–
  From here to retirement.

  Bibliography: p.
  1. Retirement—United States—Planning.
  2. Retirement income—United States—Planning.
  3. Aged—United States—Life skills guides.
  4. Self-actualization (Psychology) I. Title.
  HQ1062.B78   1988   646.7′9   87-34511
  ISBN 0-8499-3119-3

89801239 RRD 987654321

Printed in the United States of America

Dedicated
with much appreciation
to Alice, who practices positive thinking,
and to our children,
Diane, Darrell, Judith, and Jana,
who help make these years the best ever.

CONTENTS

LIST OF ILLUSTRATIONS

Figures

Tables

FOREWORD

From Here to Retirement is everything a book on retirement living should be—informative, entertaining, and best of all readable. Financial advice, psychological advice, good words on how to remain active—a person following Paul Brown's prescription should be able to remain healthy, at least moderately wealthy, and wise through his or her retirement years.

Mr. Brown has obviously given a lot of thought to his book and knows of what he speaks. As more and more of our people join the ranks of the retirees, and a greater percentage of Americans' lifespans are devoted to retirement, interest in retirement is growing all the time. I know this book will be consulted frequently by those who have already retired, or who are planning to do so in the near future.

CLAUDE PEPPER, Chairman
U.S. House of Representatives
Select Committee on Aging

INTRODUCTION

At some point during their career years, most people dream about the freedom and fulfillment retirement will bring—no more fighting rush-hour traffic, more time for leisure pursuits and travel, and the opportunity for exciting new adventures. But actually experiencing the personal fulfillment one dreams about is something else entirely—something too important to leave to chance.

In the following pages, I show how to live out your dreams by energizing them with good planning and preparation. You will learn how to use your here-and-now to insure abundant living in those years beyond your present career. It's your choice. You can make your dreams come true or watch them evaporate in the heat of reality. Proper preparation makes the difference.

Some retired people are bushwhacked by boredom or depression while others live zestful and meaningful later years because they prepared for these years long before they cut the umbilical line from their career. In this book I cover two basic areas of preparation for a successful retirement: the material side such as finances and the choice of a place to live; and the mental and spiritual side, the emotions and attitudes. How you deal with one affects your success in dealing with the other. They are inseparable.

I have also included a variety of information and suggestions about the primary concerns that confront the would-be retiree:

▶ A blueprint for determining your future financial needs and building a secure financial future.

▶ Ways to develop winning attitudes that provide your motive power.

▶ A strategy for personal growth and fulfillment.

▶ How-tos for coping with difficult adjustments in marriage and personal identity.

▶ Suggestions on how to decide where you will live.

▶ Tables and worksheets to guide you and encourage you to start your motor and begin your journey.

▶ Notes and an extended bibliography that invite you to explore further your special interests.

It has been my goal to make this book a life resource—a repository of useful ideas to which you may refer from time to time in the years before and during retirement. It is my fervent hope that my efforts will help prevent wrinkles in your later-life scenario.

From my own "sweet and sour" transition into this stage of life, I learned much about what works and what doesn't. But even more informative were the real-life adventures of helpful, loving friends. Some soared like powerful eagles and some crashed. Their sometimes humorous, sometimes poignant flights flavor the wisdom extracted from their experiences. To them I am most grateful for their willingness to share their stories. I have changed names and minor details to insure their anonymity.

My special thanks also go to my wife, Alice, and Jim Hewett, who read my manuscript and made helpful suggestions that kept me headed in the right direction, and to Randy Morris of

Marathon Financial Advisors and attorney Diane Brown, who contributed to the validity of the financial sections. I greatly appreciate the patient efforts of Beverly Phillips, my editor at Word, who honed the rough edges of my prose, helping to clarify ideas and making them more readable.

So what can you expect? *From Here to Retirement* is a book of challenge and encouragement to help you prepare now to make your retirement dreams come true—a guidebook that will help you discover rich opportunities for personal growth and fulfillment in the years that lie beyond your present career.

CHAPTER ONE

POISED ON THE EDGE
OF ADVENTURE

The blare of the TV met Helen's ears as she returned from shopping that afternoon. In the living room she could see the top of Vince's head above the back of the overstuffed chair, a bag of corn chips on one side and a six pack of beer on the other. When he did not respond to her "Hi," she walked around in front of him. Still in his bathrobe, three days' scraggly gray beard on his face, mouth sagging, he was seeing nothing. Vince was dead.

Shocking. When Vince retired eight months before, the company gave him a thorough physical exam and pronounced him in excellent health for a sixty-five-year-old, predicting a life expectancy of eighty-one years. He was ecstatic. Thinking in terms of continuous leisure, Vince pictured a very happy future. But he found he couldn't fish all the time and he soon ran out of projects around the house. Having developed no other engrossing interest outside of his work, he seemed befuddled and unable to think of anything worth doing.

One morning several weeks after he retired, Helen questioned his unkempt appearance. "Why shave?" he asked. "I'm not going anywhere."

Helen, busy with her own activities, hardly noticed when Vince decided not to dress in the morning. But later she realized that he shaved and dressed only on those rare days he had something to do. He was knee-deep in the swamp of depression.

Many retirees go through a period of depression before they get their act together. This story is a composite of three men I have known. Vince (not his real name) died. The other two suffered health problems but muddled through and finally emerged much wiser.

Evidence has piled up over the years that poor health and sometimes death follow closely a sudden shift from a satisfactory career to a dreamless, planless retirement. Stripped of his work, Vince had no dream, no plans, no challenge, no absorbing interest, no hope.

ACTIVATING THE BIG DREAM

Realizing any big dream demands a certain energetic aliveness, a zest for living that I call active expectancy. Just as positive expectations are powerful energizers, negative expectations are de-energizers. Expect nothing and you will probably get it. On the other hand, expect much and you open yourself to the power of belief.

Positive expectations do not, of themselves, guarantee the excitingly satisfying life. Not even in retirement. But they can stimulate and motivate us to action.

Often when we think of our life beyond middle age, our minds tend to lock up on finances and health. Important as they are there is something else that really determines our happiness. The power that can gild these years with a golden glitter is in our attitudes. Successful retirement, as with any big change in life, is as much an inner journey as an outer change. The really tough problems in retirement are those of the mind and spirit, the emotions and attitudes. How we resolve these makes the difference between languishing and living.

» Bill and Margaret «

Bill knows that, and he has a dream. In his mid fifties, tall, tan, and robust, he would be at ease in a ten-gallon hat and western jeans astride a horse. His "aw shucks" personality wraps an iron core of confidence and determination. No longer on the ranch where he was raised, Bill is now an urbanite holding a responsible position with a large corporation. As we talk, he tells me that he is facing the possibility of little or no retirement benefits from his financially troubled employer.

"Doesn't that worry you?" I ask. A pause, a smile, and then he responds, "Let me answer that as I show you around the place."

We walk through lush vegetables in his terraced garden as he describes his self-designed watering system attached to his own well and future plans. "More gardens over here . . . a greenhouse there . . . a processing facility . . ." Bill's words and ideas tumble over each other like romping puppies. His enthusiasm for growing things is undeniable.

Later, while Bill is in the kitchen making tea, his wife, Margaret, informs me that he doesn't always have his head and hands in the soil. The two of them are also interested in the theater and travel and are already enjoying those activities.

Bringing the tea into the living room, Bill rejoins the discussion. He says, "Margaret and I have been very frugal. And, like everyone else, we've made some financial mistakes. But our conservative investing has paid off, and I am personally managing our modest real-estate investments. Even without a pension, we will have an adequate income and certainly plenty of food. If I do get a pension, it will just be frosting on the cake. I can hardly wait till I have more time to try out some of my other plans."

Bill is well on his way to a successful retirement because he is willing to pay the price to make his dreams come true. You can do the same. Regardless of what your life has been up to now, you, too, can slip into a wonderful new world in your later years. This stage of life presents a unique opportunity for satisfaction and self-fulfillment.

But how? How can we experience autumn years that are a profoundly fulfilling adventure?

First we must ask ourselves:

What is really important?
What do we expect from life?
What do we expect of ourselves?

Expect much; dream big. Blessed are those who dream big dreams and are willing to pay the price to make them come true.

SOARING OR CRASHING:
IT'S YOUR CHOICE

Consider the words *freedom* and *liberty*. Let your imagination soar as the meaning of those words tantalize your mind with visions of fulfillment you may have thought impossible. Freedom from commuting, the boss, the eight-to-five grind. Freedom to travel, relax, play, pursue other interests, develop new skills, volunteer, and spend more time with your family.

Only a few years ago the terms *later years* and *retired* implied negative ideas like worn-out, incapable, done with, obsolete, and discarded. Now a more accurate concept of those terms can be summed up in one word—*liberated.*

The ominous retirement scene of the early and mid 1970s is well documented. Research by Tony Lamb, government agencies, and others painted a frightening picture of many retirees with serious problems—financial, physical, and psychological.[1]

For some people, retirement has been the pits. But times are changing. Recent studies such as that by the Teachers Insurance and Annuity Association show that the majority of retirees now are satisfied with their retirement. A closer look at the survey reveals that the people who said they did the most preparation for retirement also were the most contented and financially secure.[2]

Fortunately, due to better retirement benefits, better health, and greater awareness of the need for preparation, more and more people are really enjoying liberation in this stage of their lives. I personally know many people who are delighted with their retirement. Enthusiastic, optimistic, and relatively worry free, they are experiencing the happiness and fulfillment which we all hope for in our vintage years. They have learned to live in terms of a continuing interest, a theme, a meaningful commitment or purpose that gives them a reason for living and a lasting feeling of self-fulfillment.

But now the rest of the story. In my research I have discovered a disillusioning malady that attacks some retirees. It is revealed in a friend's account of his experiences during his first four years of retirement.

» Jack «

Jack, an accomplished golfer with an agreeable wife, moved to Southern California to pursue his dream of the perfect retirement—year around golf. He joined several golf groups and played four or five times a week, sometimes six if an out-of-town friend showed up unexpectedly. Loving the challenge of improving his score, the camaraderie, new golf courses, and socializing at the nineteenth hole, he was very happy. His wife had her own interests and didn't hassle him about jobs around the house unless there was something serious like a leaky dishwasher.

Two years later when I visited Jack, our conversation turned to retirement. With a pensive expression on his face, he shifted into his philosophical mode.

"You know, Paul," he confessed, "I never believed it could happen, but I'm tired of golf."

"You've got to be kidding."

"No, I'm serious," he continued. "Golf has lost its attraction. I reached my peak about a year ago, and then my game just seemed to fall apart. I even took some lessons which helped for a while. My game is up one week and down the next. But after thinking about it, I realize it's not just that I can't improve my game. It's mostly in my head. It took me a long time to admit to myself that I'm actually bored with golf. It has no excitement or challenge for me any more. Is there such a thing as a burned-out golfer?"

We kicked that question around without arriving at an answer and finally I asked, "Now what? What are you going to do in place of golf?"

He rambled a bit, and it was obvious that he hadn't solved that problem. Jack had never developed any interests outside of golf—nothing, that is, that seemed important and meaningful. He had previously thought of retirement only in terms of play. Now he is having to sort out his feelings and search for something else.

This is not an isolated case. I found others who launched into retirement bright-eyed and bushy-tailed with the feeling that happiness and unending recreation were synonymous. After a year or two of nothing but fun and games, disillusionment descended on them like a black shroud. Play is great and I highly recommend it. But most people need both play and something else. All play is a little like too much candy. Life tends to lose its flavor and become meaningless. People without a purpose begin to ask, "Is this all there is?" These are the ones who have not discovered what's really important or what it is that makes life meaningful and fulfilling. Nor have they learned to think of later years as a time for mental and spiritual growth to enrich their lives.

So it seems that in retirement, we can either soar to the heights of new adventure and growth or crash like a ruptured hot-air balloon. How can we assure ourselves of the former?

SAVE YOUR LIFE
WITH FLIGHT TRAINING

First of all we need some flight training—some future planning—that will prepare us for successful retirement. It's only natural for us to be a bit nervous when we contemplate the changes that retirement will bring. But finances are the first concerns for most of us. Through the years we have clawed our way through the rigors of financial survival training. As members of the debt set, we have been battered by recurring cycles of recession and inflation. Many of our checking accounts need month-to-month resuscitation.

Our minds won't let us forget our experiences, so we ask ourselves if retirement can possibly be any different. Are we really prepared to fly—to soar into the wild blue yonder of happy retirement?

The answer is complex. Certainly financial concerns are valid, but they are not the only considerations. Often mental, emotional, and health problems emerge from relative obscurity like an unseen wind shear, destroying the lift on our wings of happiness and contentment. Our finances, the place we live, and our relationships may be exactly what we want and we can still be miserable. Whatever fosters real happiness and contentment in any stage of life will do the same in our later years. The problem is that, at this stage, we are making some system-shocking changes in our lives to which we must adjust.

Many people, myself included, have been chagrined and baffled by some of the surprises that crop up in retirement. Through my own experiences and interviews with many retirees, I have gained a broad perspective—viewpoints from every conceivable angle. Not at all surprising is the fact that, having traveled the route, our hindsight is vastly superior to our foresight.

One thing is certain; financial seminars offered to older workers are not adequate preparation for retirement. My wife and I attended a typical one just one year before my retirement. Concentrating exclusively on financial aspects, it was a very good seminar, presenting valuable financial information by knowledgeable people. But for people on the verge of retirement, it was too little too late.

Often planned and presented by younger people who have not experienced retirement, these late-life financial seminars merely verify your financial situation, good or bad. You either have or haven't done the right things. Trying to correct your mistakes at that late date is about as effective as a quarterback trying to redirect a poorly thrown pass in mid flight. Body English won't do it.

Fortunately for us, years before, Alice and I had taken most of the right financial steps. Those who hadn't could only sadly observe what they should have done twenty years earlier. In many cases, the only solution was to delay retirement until the financial can of worms could be untangled.

What people need is comprehensive retirement training starting at age fifty or earlier: a multi-session program broad in scope. It should consider all aspects of retirement including financial, psychological, medical, and legal. Such a program should be made available to people at least ten years before they retire. Twenty years would be better.

It is shocking to realize how poorly our American industry and government are meeting this need. One of the most successful programs of retirement planning is in Europe where a course of six weekly sessions is organized several times a year. Lectures are given by experts on the medical, legal, economic, social, and spiritual problems of retirement. Yet, according to the eminent Swiss physician, Dr. Paul Tournier, the first experiments in preparatory courses for retirement were made in America.[3]

Too many people take off on their retirement flight with a very poor flight plan and no training. Encountering fog and turbulence, they lose control and splatter themselves all over the retirement countryside. With good planning and training, most in-flight problems can be avoided, and those that are encountered can be confidently confronted and vanquished.

PLANNING WITH PURPOSE AND DIRECTION

It was on my fiftieth birthday that I suddenly became aware of how much of my own mortality had already been spent. The years ahead needed some thoughtful attention. Would they be a happy, satisfying stage in my life?

Some people think of retirement as a time to park and turn off the engine. A word of caution here: Retirement may mean stopping work, but ceasing activity? Never! If you stop, you'll rust.

One of my friends is a stickler for definitions. When he asked me how I define retirement, I was stumped. But only in the sense that I can't define it in one sentence. It's different things to different people. Retirement may be a time for leisure and travel. One might change careers, work part time, or stop employment altogether to devote oneself to other pursuits such as volunteer work or a hobby.

But this autumn-years-stage is more than that. It is more a state of mind than a state of non-employment. It is a time to reflect on the purpose of life, to redirect our lives and invest skills and experience in new directions. Instead of being preoccupied with self, we can turn to new forms of usefulness and service to others. We can begin something different; be our own boss; grow as a human being, mentally and spiritually.

It is important, however, to start this growing process while still in the prime of life. Dr. Tournier declares:

> Your manner of life now is already determining your life in those years of old age and retirement, without your realizing it even, and perhaps without your giving enough thought to it.[4]

Satisfactory retirement is a process rather than an event. It is a transition from one stage of life to another. To be right for you, it must be a very personal and individually unique thing, not something programmed by someone else. The purpose of this book is to help you determine what you want out of retirement and how to get it.

As you prepare for this transition, remember that you will not only be retiring *from* something; but more significantly, you will be retiring *to* something. And you can make it an adventure that has all the color of a New England autumn.

CHAPTER TWO

THE REAL WORLD OF MONEY MATTERS

Byron had it made. Following the advice of his mail-order financial advisory service, his stock investments had ridden the rampaging bull market to the heights of euphoria. But suddenly Black Monday plunged the stock market into the crash of 1987. The only response from his advisory service was "Oops, we missed it." But to Byron, it meant much more than a ho-hum "oops." The convulsive drop in stock prices had cracked his nest egg.

Planning to retire at age sixty-two, Byron, now fifty-eight years old, had been ready to start selling some of his stocks and investing the proceeds in fixed income securities and deferred fixed annuities. With that income when he retired, along with his modest pension, he and Leona could maintain their standard of living. Now with the 25-percent drop in the value of his stocks, it was either retire later or suffer a decreased standard of living.

Byron felt defeated, but he didn't panic. He and Leona decided it was time for a heart-to-heart talk with a financial counselor. They obtained names of local financial planners from the Institute of Certified Financial Planners (ICFP) as well as referrals from trusted friends. Checking references and credentials, they found a financial planner who was also a Registered Investment Advisor. He was competent and had been in the business locally for twelve years; his reputation was impeccable.

When Byron and Leona found out what marvelous results they could expect from good money management, they were almost glad the stock market had tumbled. By selecting and following up on some of the actions suggested by the planner, they will realize their dream.

Others have not been so lucky. Basing plans entirely on projections of economic trends without paying attention to management of your assets is risky business. (Bullfighting is probably safer.) The very nature of all the elements that make up an economy, the impact of millions of randomly distributed human actions and government actions, both domestic and foreign, make the job of accurate forecasting very difficult. In fact, it's not unusual for crystal-ball gazers in our economic system to eventually "eat ground glass." And yet, in financial matters as in any other kind of planning, the better our estimate of future conditions, the better our planning.

Thus we are hoisted on the horns of a dilemma. The perfect plan can result only from perfect forecasting, which is impossible. But we can reduce the negative impact of inaccurate forecasting by crafting a financial plan that will produce good (not perfect) results in any financial weather.

But first let's orient ourselves to face the real world of money matters.

UNSCRAMBLING THE STATISTICAL MESSAGE

Sooner or later all retirement discussions arrive at the gut issue—M-O-N-E-Y. And out come the horror stories about pensions and medical insurance that are either inadequate or nonexistent—stories about people who enter the ranks of retirees in a financial condition that ranges from a barely adequate existence to dog-food poverty. Often these stories are true, but it's important to remember that statistics change.

For example, prior to 1984 the U.S. Department of Labor gave these frightening statistics: "Today, of every 100 people who reach age 65, only two are financially independent; 23 must continue working, and 75 must depend on friends, charity, or relatives. Of every 100 Americans reaching age 65 today, a horrifying 96 are flat broke."[1]

Although these statistics were true at one time, they are now obsolete. However, they are still being cited by people who have an ax to grind or a product to sell.

Picking up mercury between your fingers would be easier than trying to sort out the real truth behind some economic statistics. Even when the statistics are correct, those who handle and report the statistics have a tendency toward selectively presenting those which support their own biases and purposes. Those who want to reduce Social Security try to prove that people drawing Social Security are affluent. Those who want to preserve Social Security try to prove that retirees are on the edge of poverty. The truth is somewhere in between. Compare the following examples.

An article in *Money Guide* (1985) states that "Of the 1794 retirees recently surveyed by the Teachers Insurance and Annuity Association, 92% said they were satisfied with retirement. A closer look at the survey reveals that the people who said they did the most preparation for retirement also were the most contented and financially secure."[2]

From the *Wall Street Journal* of December 19, 1985, come these statements:

> Fifteen years ago, one quarter of aged Americans lived in poverty—twice the rate of the general populations. Today the poverty rate for the elderly has been halved; at 12.4% last year, it was lower for them than the 14.4% rate for Americans over-all.[3]

Another article in the *Wall Street Journal* of December 26, 1985, throws a little more light on the rather blurred financial picture of retired people:

> Without Social Security, more than half of the elderly would have incomes below the poverty level. . . . While many elderly indeed are comfortable, poverty is pervasive among the 6.2 million older Americans who rely on Social Security for 90% or more of their income.[4]

Not only is the retirement picture blurry, but it is continually changing. In another *Wall Street Journal* article (August 26, 1987), Gregory Stricharchuk writes about pension benefits other than Social Security:

> Already the number of Americans with pension coverage is shrinking, after climbing steadily for thirty years. In 1981, more than 45 percent of American workers were covered by retirement plans, up from just 22 percent in 1950. But by 1985, the most recent year for which figures are available, the percentage had slipped to 43 percent, according to the Employee Benefit Research Institute in Washington, D.C.[5]

This means that, to a statistician who looks at nothing but numbers, Social Security gives an illusion of elderly affluence that isn't necessarily true. Many of these Social Security recipients who are thrown over the statistical fence into a greener pasture are still on the edge of poverty. Social Security, even though it pushes you out of the poverty category, doesn't make you rich.

Other data and my own direct observations show that there are many affluent seniors. And, between the affluent and those on the edge of poverty, there are many levels of comfort (or discomfort). But just what the percentages are depends on the definitions you use, the data base you select, and how you slice the data. Whatever your bias is, you can support it with statistics. But one thing seems certain; the financial condition of the elderly is improving.

And, for the purposes of this book, the essential issue is that no matter what the statistics say, you can design your own financial fate. The sooner you start, the better the results. Without a doubt, good planning at any age will be of some benefit. But to assure yourself financially secure later years, it's necessary to start planning early in your career. The need for careful planning is more apparent than ever when you consider that you are likely to live after retirement as many years as you did before you began working.

Now let's see if we can make some "cents" out of economic reality.

VERBAL SMOKE HIDES
FINANCIAL TRAPS

Unless some strange set of circumstances seals us off from the outside world, we are continually bombarded with facts and ideas that have economic significance—new bills passed or being considered by Congress, OPEC meetings, politicians making speeches, economists making predictions, gold bugs crying "doom," and self-styled financial wizards selling their advisory services.

What's a person to believe? Our minds get batted around like tether balls until they are wound up in tighter and tighter circles. With so many information sources inputting to our mental computers, it is very difficult to separate truth from fiction. I'm not talking here about the truth of future predictions. I'm talking about how hard it is to see the reality of present, here-and-now, financial truth through this verbal smoke screen.

The economy and financial markets have sustained great changes in recent years. They have become more volatile. The markets offer more new and modified financial products every day. The velocity of money, the rate at which it flows through the economy, has been increased by electronic transfers and other means. Government policies and actions have had, and will continue to have, a powerful influence.

For example, the new tax law of 1986 will mean complex changes for many who will, no doubt, need to redirect their financial strategy. And, depending on where they are financially, it may have a profound effect on their welfare, as may any future changes. Furthermore, whatever the cause of the October 1987 stock-market spasm, it has dropped us back to reality from unwarranted euphoria. Opinions vary sharply over the meaning of the event. But people respond in whatever manner appears to be in their best interest and only time will reveal the economic impact.

The point is simply that, because of new laws and various other reasons, the economic climate is constantly changing. Therefore, as you begin to plan for your retirement, keep in mind that your own personal situation may change through outside influences. Consequently, you may, from time to time, find it worthwhile to change your financial strategy. For example, your choice of investments may be affected. Some of the current investment products, particularly those emphasizing tax sheltering, may well disappear. Others may become less attractive. New investment products, spawned by the new tax law, are coming on the market. Some are good, some are bad. In other words, your financial plan must be flexible. To be realistic and useful, it must be revised periodically. I recommend updating it at least every two years up to age fifty-five, then once a year thereafter.

A good financial plan is a very personal thing, tailored to the circumstances, wishes, and temperament of the individual or couple. Because of the variables—economic and personal—it would make no sense at all for me to recommend specific investments in this book. Instead, my purpose is to emphasize principles of investing (what to look for in a good investment and what to avoid) and the characteristics of different investments (what return to expect, advantages and disadvantages, and the levels of risk to look for).

Regardless of how you go about planning your financial future, be realistic. Don't be mesmerized by money mythology. We all cherish our own wish list concerning the economy, interest rates, and our own financial situation. But wishing alone will not make it so.

Now let's examine some caveats. These are not all-inclusive, just basic examples of the alligators lurking in the financial swamp:

▶ If you are made an offer that sounds too good to be true, it is.

▶ If anyone claims that some investment has no risk, run, don't walk, to the nearest exit. There is no such thing as a risk-free investment, except, perhaps, in the land of Oz.

▶ Financial advisors and other professional help should be selected very carefully after thoroughly reviewing their qualifications and references.

▶ Economic predictions by economists and financial advisors should be taken with a generous dose of skepticism. At any given time, many of them will be wrong.

▶ Risks are steep where tax shelters are deep.

▶ A financial guru can be dangerous to your wealth. It can be very risky to put the control of your assets in the hands of someone else.

We will talk more about these and other caveats later in this chapter and the next. The good news is that the hidden financial traps can be avoided. Not only that, but proper planning will mitigate the bad effects of changes in the economic situation and laws. By hedging your decisions and taking other precautions, you will have a good supply of money and a better chance of making your retirement dreams come true.

SOCIAL SECURITY AND
YOUR COMPANY BENEFITS

Social Security won't do it all. Designed to be only a piece of your retirement cake, it will not make you fat. If you like to eat three square meals a day, you need a bigger stash in your pantry. Indeed, Social Security may, in future years, bear no resemblance to its present form. Changes are impossible to forecast. But putting all your eggs in a Social Security cake could leave you with a bad case of financial undernourishment. Of course, this is not to say that you shouldn't get everything you can from Social Security.

People with other pensions, in addition to whatever Social Security they may qualify for, often find that these are also insufficient—if not at first, then later. Failure to consider the uncertainties of pensions, the effects of inflation, and the impact of other contingencies may result in unpleasant surprises. Most nongovernment pensions are nonescalating, that is, they do not have a built-in inflation factor. Although the future rate of inflation will, no doubt, vary widely from year to year, most economic experts agree that, over the long run, inflation will be very much a part of our human existence. This means that to keep up with cost-of-living increases you will need to add some bricks to your financial foundation.

Generalizing about pensions and company savings plans is as useless as a snow shovel in Tahiti. Companies' retirement plans differ as much as their balance sheets. Furthermore, recent years have brought rapid changes—generally for the better. Becoming popular in some companies are so-called cafeteria plans which allow you to select those benefit options that fit your particular needs. A pension combined with company-sponsored savings plan and other types of benefits can be an impressive cornerstone for the retirement structure.

Learn all you can about your own company's pension, savings plan, and associated retirement benefits. This includes understanding how your company computes its pensions when you become vested, what benefits you can expect and at what age, whether your company will reduce your pension by the amount of your Social Security benefits, and the type of survivors pension benefit your spouse may receive.

There may be many goodies stashed in your company's benefit bag—possibilities in which you may already be participating such as profit-sharing plans, 403(b) accounts, tax deferring 401(k) plans, employee stock-ownership plans (ESOPS), and payroll based employee stock-ownership plans (PAYSOPS). The 401(k) plan is a tax-deferred savings plan set up by an employer. Employee contributions to the plan come out of his/her salary before taxes are computed. No tax is paid until the money is distributed, normally after retirement. The 403(b) plan is the same kind of plan, but it's only for employees of nonprofit organizations or government jobs. This, of course, would include school system employees.

There are Keogh plans for the self-employed and, of course, IRAs (Individual Retirement Accounts) for anyone under 70½ who gets paid for working. (For taxpayers covered by a pension plan, the 1986 tax law imposes new restrictions on 1987-and-on IRA contributions. However, the interest on the IRA is still tax deferred.)

Company benefits such as those just listed and others can be a veritable gold mine. Survey the entire company mine and decide which are the richest veins for you to work.

Here are some of the questions about your employer's benefits for which you should get answers:

▶ What benefit options do you have?
▶ How much can you contribute to the available plans?
▶ What is your employer's contribution?
▶ When will your employer's contributions belong to you?
▶ Can you borrow or withdraw some of these contributions before retirement?

▶ What are the tax consequences now and later?

▶ How early can you get a pension?

▶ What is the reduction in benefits if you retire early?

▶ Does your employer provide special incentives for early retirement?

▶ Is your employer's pension fund solid or shaky?

▶ If you leave the company for a time and return, can you pick up your benefit plans where they were when you left?

Those people who find it necessary or desirable to change companies need to keep in mind that the more often they change the less likely they'll get much of a pension, if any at all.

Many companies continue a portion of your company-paid life insurance and medical insurance during retirement. Usually these vary depending on whether you are under or over 65, at which time Medicare becomes available to those who qualify. Some companies sponsor Medicare supplemental insurance. But in many cases this insurance is inadequate. Be sure to find out the details of any such insurance and investigate several other plans. The American Association of Retired Persons (AARP) has a smorgasbord of good plans which you should compare with others.

The important thing is that, when you get the data, you make a timely decision. After you've jumped out of the airplane, it's too late to go back for your parachute.

ESTIMATING BENEFITS
AT RETIREMENT

When your head and notebook are crammed with information about your retirement benefits, you can engage in some educated guesswork. First, you will need to project your pension and savings to the date (age) at which you want to retire, taking into account expected salary increases. Using your company formulas, unleash your handy-dandy, desk-top computer and crunch the numbers. Actually your company will probably do it for you at your request. And some companies do the projections every year as a policy, furnishing each worker with a copy of his/her own personal data.

This is an imprecise but important exercise. The younger you are the more imprecise will be the projections, but also the more time you have to make adjustments. By age fifty-five the figures will become more accurate.

Now comes the fun. If you are not too mystified by numbers and the operation of a calculator, you can play some "what if" games to ascertain the results of contributing different amounts to various savings plans. If this boggles your mind too much, you can secure help from a good financial planner or accountant who will create these projections for you based on the information you furnish.

For an estimate of your Social Security benefits, simply fill out a request card and mail or deliver it to your nearest Social Security office. (These cards are usually available at your company personnel office as well as directly from Social Security offices.) Once your Social Security benefits have been computed, the information will be mailed to you.

Estimating your benefits at retirement is just the beginning. There are other projections that you will need to make. For example, what kind of retirement income will you need.

HOW TO FIGURE OUT
WHAT YOU WILL NEED

What retirement income would make you feel good—not ecstatic, just good? Or maybe you would prefer to feel ecstatic. If you are still twenty years away from retirement, you may think that this is an exercise in futility. An estimate at that stage will, of course, be just an educated guess. But the closer you get to retirement, the more accurate will be your estimates. So don't worry that your first figures may be unreal.

To help you focus in on these numbers, prepare a current budget, if you don't already have one. What are you currently spending? Include everything. This will be the base from which you will project your spending pattern during retirement.

Few people have the financial resources to replace their salaries completely and few need to anyway. Some expenses dwindle or disappear in retirement. Some typical reductions are:

▶ commuting costs

▶ housing costs (your mortgage may be paid off)

▶ dependent support (education, etc.)

▶ Social Security payments

▶ auto expenses

▶ installment purchases

▶ interest payments (smaller charge accounts for example)

▶ life insurance (less coverage with children gone)

▶ entertainment and travel expenses (senior discounts).

There may be others of course. Or perhaps my list doesn't fit your situation. This just goes to show that you should make your own list. To show you what I mean, let's look for a moment at entertainment and travel. Despite senior discounts, your overall cost for these may actually go up if, in retirement, you choose to do more entertaining and traveling.

"Obvious," you say. But there are other not-so-obvious expenses that may balloon, too. One of the most common mistakes is underestimating financial needs and desires during retirement. You can be lulled into an intellectual stupor by articles written by people who haven't yet retired. These writers are more apt to emphasize the reduction in expenses without telling you about the expenses that are likely to increase.

Before we get into the details of likely increases, let's consider a generalization that can be useful in your early planning. This should be used only as a base from which to start and can be replaced with more precise numbers later.

Money Guide says that you can expect to maintain your pre-retirement standard of living with an income between 60 percent and 80 percent of your former pre-tax earnings. Other estimates run between 55 percent and 70 percent. So it is clear that the estimates are somewhat squishy. However, one thing is almost certain. The higher your pre-retirement income, the smaller the percentage you can use in your calculations. Studies have found that the retirement living expenses of the higher-earning worker are usually a proportionately lower percentage of his working pay than the retirement living expenses of the lower-earning worker.

Stanley Cohen, a financial planner and senior vice president for the brokerage firm of Moseley, Hallgarten, Estabrook & Weeden in New York City, says a worker earning $70,000 or more should aim for a replacement rate of 60 percent, while someone grossing $30,000 or less ought to aim for 80 percent.[6]

Having thus generalized, let's consider some of the expenses that may increase. Depending on your health, you may have high *medical bills* or at least the added expense of paying for your own health insurance. Small and medium-sized companies rarely pay health insurance premiums for their retirees. Large companies sometimes pay health insurance for early retirees up to the time that Medicare takes over at age sixty-five. Sometimes they even have a supplemental insurance after age sixty-five, but it may be inadequate. Regardless, medical costs, whether bills or insurance premiums, often increase in retirement.

Although *housing expenses* such as mortgage payments may cease or dwindle, your old house may be in need of some major repairs. Common problems are a worn-out heating system, plumbing in need of major renovation, and a leaky roof that gives you your morning shower in bed. Painting and other periodic maintenance needs do not magically disappear. And if you decide to live somewhere else, what will housing cost there?

Children or aging parents may need your help.

What kind of *inheritance,* if anything, do you want to leave your heirs?

Would you like to make other *bequests* to your church or a favorite charity?

And don't forget *inflation.* Rumors of the death of inflation are premature.

So much for some of the possible increased expenses. Your circumstances may compel other expenditures not considered here. With these as a starter, make your own list.

But who among you is content with just basic necessities? Let's kick around some of your big dreams. Such things as travel to exotic places or some not so exotic. Hobbies. Sports. And don't forget your spouse. If you have an expensive hobby like flying your own airplane, he/she may demand equal indulgence. And be generous with yourself and your spouse. For purposes of planning, it pays to aim high.

With these numbers guestimated, you are now ready to prepare a retirement budget. Comparing this budget with your present budget will help you ascertain just what retirement income you should shoot for. Preparation and discussion of these numbers will provide endless opportunities for communication with your spouse. Forms to help you can usually be obtained from financial planners, accountants, or stationery stores. One very good guide is put out by Touche Ross and Co., a CPA firm headquartered in New York, but with branch offices in many areas.[7]

PAINTING YOUR FINANCIAL PICTURE

Some years ago, my friend, Rolf, started a business. It was a music store, and two years later it seemed to be going along so well that he thought friends might be interested in helping expand. I was interested, so I asked for a copy of his latest balance sheet. He didn't have one but said he would prepare one. Three weeks later, a chagrined Rolf came to me and said, "You wouldn't want to see my balance sheet. I've been losing money all year and didn't even know it." In a financial sense, no one had been minding the store.

You may think it's highly unlikely that someone would not know his/her financial status, but it's really not too unusual for nonbusiness people to be broke and not know it. All of which leads to some recommendations. Whether or not you act as your own financial planner, there are two basic things you should do:

1. Learn how to blow away the fog from your financial landscape so you can paint an accurate picture of it. When you really understand your finances, the fog dissipates and the sun shines through. You can see where you're headed and decide whether you should change direction. One navigation instrument used for this is commonly called a balance sheet. It lists all assets and liabilities, and gives your net worth on the bottom line, which is what you have to work with.

2. Write out your financial goals. On your first try, you may be as uncertain as a teen-age boy on his first date. But that's okay. Practice will bring a feeling of confidence. And you will get plenty of practice because you should frequently update your short-, medium-, and long-term goals. A good financial planner can help you focus in on some appropriate goals.

STRATEGY FOR FILLING THE GAP

You are now ready to find out if your expected retirement income will satisfy your spending requirements—whether you will have a surplus or a deficit. Begin by filling out figure 2.1. If

Table 2.1

Life Expectancy Calculations in Years

Present Age	Years Remaining
40	37
45	33
50	28
55	24
60	20
65	17

there is a gap between what you need and what you expect to have from your presently projected assets, it will show up on line 14.

For these calculations, you need to estimate how long you will live. If you are in normal health, use national mortality numbers which, for your convenience, I have shown in table 2.1. These averages can be used for both men and women.[8] This is the number you should use in line 6 of figure 2.1. Such a number gives you a margin of safety, too, because each year's savings will begin to earn a return from the investments you put them in.

You are now ready to do some serious figuring. The worksheet in figure 2.1 will guide you in making these calculations.

The multipliers used in the calculations provide a built-in inflation adjustment. They assume your savings will earn 3 percent after inflation and taxes, both before and after you retire.

For line 2 use the retirement income you estimated you would need or a percentage of line 1 as indicated. If your gross earnings are now less than $50,000, use a figure toward the high end of the line 2 percentage range—55 to 80 percent.

For line 3a, get an estimate from Social Security. Married couples with one salaried spouse should increase those figures 50 percent. For line 3b, get an estimate from your employer.

1. Current annual income $_____

2. Annual retirement income needed in
   1988 dollars $_____
   (55 to 80% of line 1 or from
   estimated retirement budget)

3. Expected annual pension income
   a. Social Security income $_____
   b. Employer pension $_____
   c. Other $_____

4. Total annual retirement pensions $_____
   (Add lines 3a, 3b, and 3c.)

5. Annual income needed from savings/
   investments $_____
   (line 2 minus line 4)

6. Amount you must save by retirement in
   1988 dollars $_____
   (line 5 multiplied by your expected life span)

7. Amount you've saved already
   a. Employer's savings programs,
      your and employer's
      contributions $_____
   b. Other savings (your equity) $_____
      (such as money funds, stocks,
      bonds, Keoghs, IRAs,
      investment real estate)

8. Total savings to date $_____
   (Add lines 7a and 7b.)

9. Growth of savings to retirement
   a. Employer's program $_____
      (line 7a times A multiplier
      in the table below)
   b. Other savings $_____
      (line 7b times A multiplier
      in the table below)

10. Total savings to date, including
    growth to retirement $_____
    (line 9a plus line 9b)

11. Amount of savings still needed $_____
    (line 6 minus line 10)

12. Amount of savings needed each year $_____
    (line 11 times B multiplier below)

13. This year's contribution to employer's
    savings plan (yours and his) $_____

14. Amount of other savings you need each year $_____
    (line 12 minus line 13)

| Number of Years | Multipliers | |
Before You Retire	A	B
5 years	1.159	.188
10 years	1.344	.087
15 years	1.558	.054
20 years	1.806	.037

Figure 2.1. Worksheet for estimating whether retirement income will satisfy expected spending requirements.

After following the other mathematical manipulations explained on the worksheet, you will eventually come to line 14. This is the amount you need to save each year.

If you will, with your present planning, have a surplus, congratulations. But it may be a very thin surplus. In that case, as you review these figures in subsequent years, you need to be alert to the possibilities of a deteriorating balance. Considering the economic realities and uncertainties and the inadequacies of many pensions, it is my opinion that everyone should plan for and work toward accumulating additional assets during his/her working years. Then, with this capital well invested, you can choose in your retirement years to spend the income from these investments or, if necessary, spend both income and a small portion of capital every year. People with a minimum retirement income may need to do the latter (spend some of their capital each year) just to maintain a reasonable standard of living. To determine this figure, you will need to calculate the allowable annual expenditure of capital based on the years you expect to live plus a safety factor of ten or more years.

Suppose, for example, that when you retire at age sixty-five you have $100,000 that you can invest in safe securities from which you can get a 7 percent return of $583 per month. But you decide that you also want to spend some of the principal (capital) to give you a better standard of living. Your life expectancy is seventeen more years to which you add ten to get twenty-seven—the number of years on which we will base our calculation.

One way to do this would be to buy treasury notes/bonds with different maturity dates, say twenty $5000 notes or bonds with maturities spread from one to twenty-seven years. Then as each one matures, put the proceeds in a money-market fund and spend both interest and capital for whatever you want. At the present time, interest on Treasury notes/bonds varies between 7 percent and 9.5 percent depending on maturity date. Assuming a 7 percent average return over a period of twenty-seven years, and spending that plus a portion of your principal, you would receive an income of about $683 per month. This would be $100 more than just spending the interest. But at the end of twenty-seven years all your capital would be gone. That's the trade-off. If you spend just the interest, you keep your capital.

This is only one of many options available. A financial planner can propose others. But with this money, be sure to stay with very low risk investments.

If there is a deficit instead of a surplus shown on line 14 of your worksheet, you have a decision to make now. Will you (1) save enough during your remaining working years to fill the gap, (2) work longer and retire later, (3) lower your retirement standard of living, or (4) a combination of the first three.

Most people choose the first alternative and accumulate additional assets through a well-planned savings and investment program. If you inherit a bundle, you will be a leg up on us less fortunate mortals. But even then, you must be able to invest and manage it wisely, which, among other things, is what we will discuss in the next chapter.

CHAPTER THREE

PERSONAL FINANCIAL PLANNING

There are more important things in life than money. But you already know that. And you certainly don't need me to tell you that money is meant to be a means to an end, not the end itself.

What we're concerned with in this aspect of retirement planning is wrapping those "more important things" in financial security. If, in your later years, you have a comfortable financial situation, you will be free of money worry. And that will release your energy for living your dreams, for helping other people, and doing other important things.

WHERE WE'RE COMING FROM

Since this book is written primarily for persons preparing for retirement, I expect readers to be somewhere between the ages of fifty and sixty-five—intelligent (occasionally frazzled) individuals with a modicum of experience in things financial. Assuming a certain amount of reader sophistication, I make no attempt to define every term or explain some of the more elementary concepts. But for those who feel a need for some of this information, there are other sources of help, including magazines and books. Three such books are *Personal Financial Planning* by Victor Hallman and Jerry S. Rosenbloom, *Planning an Estate* by Harold Weinstock, and *Fundamentals of Insurance* by Robert I. Mehr.

Nothing in this book should be construed as a specific recommendation for a specific individual. My intent is to display the products, not to sell them. The decision to take any particular action or buy a product must be yours alone, based on your unique situation and temperament. If you want specific advice, work it out with your financial advisor or other appropriate professional.

You may still be contributing to your kids' education, but the odds are that most people in this age bracket have slipped out from under that burden. Even so, like other parents with college bills in their recent past, you may be uncomfortably close to retirement with little in the bank. In your favor, however, is the likelihood that you are at the peak of your earning power with the possibility of squirreling away money in employer-sponsored savings plans—some tax deferred—or IRAs or a self-employment Keogh.

Generally, at this stage of your life, with maximum earnings and diminishing expenses, good management of your resources will usher you into a secure retirement without bending your standard of living. But beware of the urge to splurge. That's a temptation, when, after years of heavy expenses, you find that your income now gives you a surprising margin for luxuries. Do your financial planning first before you let a spending hemorrhage wipe you out. At this stage, the secret to financing a happy retirement is controlling cash flow.

Good management is the key. But unless you have been doing it and liking it, financial planning may seem as forbidding as the Matterhorn in a blizzard. Some people will want continuous professional help. Others will manage their assets themselves. Almost everyone, whether they have a small piggy bank or a massive treasure chest will need professional advice at some point. Your need for help will depend more on you than on the size of your gold pile: how much you know, how much you are willing to learn, and how you feel about managing your money.

Let me hasten to add a word of caution here, for you can be overly dependent on advice. So regardless of the amount of help you choose, gain as much knowledge as you can about financial matters, yours in particular. Then let your own experience and good judgment guide you. Common sense applies as well to your finances as to your life work.

HOW TO SELECT PROFESSIONAL HELP

Keep one rule uppermost in your mind. Do not turn over control of your assets to anyone. Turning over everything to so-called financial wizards and forgetting about it can be a recipe for disaster. My disaster file is crammed with examples of people who have done that (some with their life savings) and deeply regretted their action. The results are often big losses, sometimes 100 percent. Some financial "gurus" are just plain incompetent; others are con artists and frauds. So no matter how much advice you seek, always keep control and decision making in your own hands.

My intent is not to scare you but rather to sharpen your awareness. There are many excellent professionals in the financial and legal communities who can help make your retirement much more enjoyable. It's just a matter of knowing how to find them and learning how to make best use of their talents.

Your financial planning should be a team effort. No one person, no matter how well-meaning, can give you expert advice in every area. The five advisors you are most likely to need are:

▶ A certified public accountant to handle tax questions and perhaps prepare tax returns.

▶ A lawyer to prepare a will and answer estate planning questions, perhaps to set up trusts for spouse and children, and any other legal questions.

▶ A money manager (or investment advisor) to give investment advice or oversee your investment portfolio.

▶ A financial planner who advises you on overall strategy and coordinates the team, making sure that each member's recommendations fit your goals which you have worked out with the help of the planner.

▶ A knowledgeable insurance agent.

Each of these advisors has a contribution to make to your welfare, but whether you use them depends on your judgment as to your need for their services. Sometimes their talents overlap. And if you use all of these experts, there must be conferences to avoid conflicts and properly coordinate their advice. There are some organizations that have all of these team members under one roof. Most individual professionals have cooperative arrangements with other professionals.

What do you, the client, have a right to expect from a professional advisor? Among the most important expectations are the following. The advisor should . . .

▶ put your best interest ahead of his own.

▶ be competent in his field.

▶ have integrity (e.g., reveal conflicts of interest and tell you when he will receive commissions on sales to you).

▶ be objective (able to understand your goals and willing to help you achieve them without trying to cram you into some other mold).

▶ present alternatives and clearly outline the advantages and disadvantages of each.

▶ word his advice in clearly understood language.

It will be necessary for you to select some of these helpers before you can be sure they have all these desirable traits. Getting referrals is one of the best ways to do this. If you can get a solid recommendation from someone in similar circumstances to yours, you're over the first hurdle. But be sure the person recommended has been in business in the area for several years and that the recommendation comes from someone you trust who has known the professional for at least two years.

You can also get referrals from professional organizations. For a financial planner, try the International Association for Financial Planning and the Institute of Certified Financial Planners; for an attorney, the local bar association. Maybe you're already working with an accountant or an attorney. They, or the first person you select for your team, can often refer you to others with whom they have worked.

When you have a list of candidates, examine and compare their qualifications and get at least three client references from each. And be sure to make up a list of questions and try to determine, in talking with the references, whether they feel the advisor meets the qualifications noted above. Check also with regulatory agencies—such as your state insurance commissioner, the Securities and Exchange Commission's (SEC) consumer affairs office, or your local Better Business Bureau—to find out if complaints have been lodged against an advisor. Find out how willing they are to consult with other members of your team when necessary. Ask for the names of other professionals they have worked with recently.

Remember that advisors are human. They cannot completely divorce themselves from their own self-interest. But that's no reason not to use them. It's a matter of understanding where they're coming from and then working within the system to get what you want. Some of the possible conflicts of interest are obvious. For example, brokers earn commissions from the stocks, bonds, insurance policies, partnerships, and other products they sell you. If they don't consider anything but the products they sell, you can well wonder whether lining their own pockets is taking precedence over nourishing your assets.

Many people who call themselves financial planners (or advisors) earn commissions from products they sell. Others are called "fee only" planners, meaning that they get a fee for the plan and advice and sell no products. Some get a planning fee as well as commissions. Any one of these with the proper qualifications and traits can do a good job for you. But I believe the "fee only" planner is much more likely to be objective and put your interests foremost. His vested interest is in pleasing you, not in making big commissions. The two of you will be leaning in the same direction.

In the financial realm there is no such thing as certainty, and that applies to selecting the right advisors. Only by their performance can you ascertain whether your advisors have been wisely chosen. Reason enough for always keeping full control of your assets in your own hands. By maintaining control, you can, with a minimum of problems, change advisors if the first selections are wrong for you. Not only that, but knowing what's going on allows you to make such a change quickly and minimize any damage.

When you have selected a planner or investment advisor and have reached the point of discussing investments, look for certain indicators of his honesty and objectivity. For example, does he discuss the risks involved in investments clearly and in detail? This information is necessary for you to decide whether an investment fits within your level of risk tolerance. When the advisor starts pushing certain investments, does he disclose the fact that he will earn commissions on whatever you buy (if indeed he will)? Does he really look in depth at all possible investments and explain why he favors certain ones and why they will help you reach your objectives?

Be very wary of any advisor who does not disclose these facts without a lot of probing on your part. If he seems prone to hide these subjects in a verbal smoke screen, he may be much more concerned with his own welfare than with yours. Look for another advisor.

A good financial planner or advisor will want to know a lot about you. So don't be alarmed if he asks probing questions. He needs to know you, your personal situation, your goals, and your financial information in complete detail. But beyond that, he also needs to understand your temperament, your level of risk tolerance, and your likes and dislikes.

As I said earlier, a good financial planner or advisor can be extremely helpful, but above all, learn as much as you can about your own financial affairs and take an active part in their management.

BUILDING YOUR FINANCIAL FOUNDATION

Company-sponsored savings plans and other types of benefits can be an impressive cornerstone for your financial foundation. But seldom will they serve as the complete structure. And many people do not have such a program. Most of us must collect other building blocks. Now let's put the first blocks in place.

Wills and Estate Planning. You may have already been harangued about the advisability of having a will and doing some estate planning. I don't intend to choreograph a long song and dance about these, although I firmly believe they are very important.

Pat was certainly glad that she and Jack had wills. This was Jack's second marriage and all the property had been acquired prior to his marriage to Pat. Twelve years and two children later, Jack died. In his will, he left everything to Pat.

If Jack had died without a will, even in the community property state where they lived, the state would have distributed the assets according to law: in this case, one-third to Pat and two-thirds to her two children. Since they are minors, the court would appoint a guardian (more attorney's fees). Pat would have to account to the court each year (each time more attorney's fees) for the use of the children's funds.

Because Jack did have a will, Pat controls all assets. The children will eventually get all the remainder after Pat dies. But in the meantime, she can take good care of herself and her children with the assets Jack left her, and (with apologies to you attorneys) at a much lower cost.

In each case, what happens without a will depends on individual circumstances and the laws of your resident state. Sad stories abound. Many knowledgeable people, including attorneys, have failed to draw up a will. Procrastination here is your worst enemy. Do it now, and your survivors will "bless" you long after you're gone.

The many legal and tax considerations make estate planning complex. It takes coordination of all the features of your estate to minimize taxes and provide adequately for your spouse and other heirs. By various devices such as trusts and holding title to assets in a particular way, you can avoid probate, save money, and maintain your privacy.

But each method of holding title has both advantages and disadvantages depending on your situation. For example, holding title to real property in joint tenancy with right of survivorship (JTROS) avoids probate. But it has income tax disadvantages that many people fail to take into account. Likewise other methods of holding title to real property have their own advantages and disadvantages. Since each person's situation is different and laws vary from state to state, you should seek professional help. Consult an attorney who specializes in estate planning and, where needed, an accountant.

Life Insurance. Usually from age fifty to age sixty-five, there is a diminishing need for life insurance for family protection.

However, even if we assume that children have been launched and that your estate will be a plump bag of goodies, there may still be reasons for some life insurance. It's usually the cheapest way to provide a comfortable income or extra luxuries for a surviving spouse. And if your estate is otherwise less than adequate, it may be the only way to protect your loved ones.

Most people who think about life insurance at this stage, have four things in mind:

1. Cash for immediate needs—expenses for final illness and burial, taxes and debts.

2. Money to pay the mortgage.

3. Readjustment money—interim funds for family members who will need time to make important decisions about moving or looking for a job.

4. Replacement income—funds to help replace the deceased's paycheck.

These are the most common reasons. If your situation is a little different, for example, you own part of or all of a business, you need advice on how to protect your interest in the business with life insurance. Your insurance agent and financial planner can help you.

If you have group life insurance, look into the possibility that such a policy can be converted to private insurance at the time of your retirement. Usually new insurance will turn out to be a better buy. But if you cannot qualify because of some medical problem, it may be better to convert the group insurance if you can do so without proof of insurability. Make your decision and take action before retirement.

If you decide that you still need some life insurance, two types worth considering are term insurance and single premium whole life. Term insurance is the cheapest pure insurance. It has no cash value, but you get the most insurance for your money.

Single premium whole life (SPWL) has become popular in the last few years. It is a big improvement over the older products such as endowment and some of the old universal life and whole life policies. It is a viable, conservative investment that provides a tax-free accumulation of competitive rate earnings (tax-deferred rather than tax-free if you cash in the policy). You have access to the accumulated cash through loans, usually at no cost, if you borrow just the earnings. The risk is that the insurance company might reduce the interest rate. If you want to bail out before the end of the early withdrawal penalty period, you would be stuck with a penalty, and have to pay tax on accumulated earnings. On your death, beneficiaries pay no tax. It's best if you intend to never cash in the policy.

The trade-off is either to buy the single premium whole life for both death benefit and tax-free accumulation of earnings, or buy the much cheaper term insurance for death benefit only and invest the premium difference elsewhere.

Another possibility is to trade in your present policies for a reduced paid-up policy or another type of life insurance, such as term, which gives you more for your money. Most policies can be switched within the same company without proof of insurability.

Don't over-dose on life insurance. If you presently have more than you need, consider cashing out some and using the money for something else. But don't drop any insurance until you are sure you can still qualify for the insurance you want.

A knowledgeable and trustworthy insurance agent can help you sort out the alternatives. The features of policies having the same name vary, and so do prices. Be sure to do some shopping around. Then talk with your planner or financial advisor to determine which alternatives best support your objectives.

Disability Insurance.   When your finances reach the point where you don't need to work, disability insurance becomes unnecessary. It's designed solely to maintain your income during periods of disability. If, during a disability, your income would still be adequate and your expected retirement benefits were still intact, disability insurance is not needed.

Medical Insurance. It's just possible that what you do about medical insurance will be among your most important retirement decisions. Unless you are very wealthy, good medical insurance is absolutely imperative for averting catastrophe and maintaining peace-of-mind in your later years.

It may come as a surprise to you that Medicare will cover only a portion of your medical bills. And that portion is diminishing. Some expenses are not covered at all and others only partially. So even after you qualify for Medicare, you will need some form of supplemental insurance to plug the holes in Medicare. But if you take timely action, you needn't worry yourself sick over the prospect of catastrophic health costs.

Many companies continue some form of medical insurance for retirees before age sixty-five, and some continue a diminished insurance at sixty-five when Medicare becomes available to those who qualify. Some companies sponsor Medicare supplemental insurance. But in many cases this insurance is inadequate. Be sure to find out the details of any such employer plan. There are also some health maintenance organizations (HMOs) worth looking into.

Most retirees will find that they have inherited the major responsibility for supplemental medical insurance. Sometimes at retirement you can convert an existing plan advantageously. But the important thing is to investigate and make your decision on medical insurance before you cut the umbilical line. Procrastination can turn retirement into a nightmare of medical bills.

Don't expect your medical insurance to pay every dollar of your expenses. The most cost-effective plans (most coverage for your money) are major medical, meaning they have deductible amounts which you pay, but they cover the big expenses. In other words, you assume more of the risk yourself so that the insurance company can charge lower premiums.

Watch out for the alligators in the medical insurance swamp. There are some unscrupulous companies and salesmen victimizing older people, selling inferior insurance and not revealing serious disadvantages of their products. The American Association of Retired Persons (AARP) sponsors a smorgasbord of good medical insurance plans. Compare their various coverage options with other companies. Most local senior centers can tell you where to get the type of information you need.

HOW TO INCREASE RETIREMENT INCOME

Part-time retirement, winding down from a full-time career to a part-time occupation, is becoming more and more popular. It's a good way to go whether you need the money or not. Some of the happiest seniors are those who have part-time jobs either as an extension of their career or in something new. In fact, if you know you or your spouse will be working part time at a known pay rate, you can subtract that amount, less taxes, from your needed savings. Be sure to take into account the tax consequences. Remember that above a certain level of earned income, depending on your age below age seventy, you begin to lose some of your Social Security payments.

In my opinion, the best of both worlds is to have enough economic resources so you don't need to work, but to work part time anyway for the love of it. Financial independence is no guarantee of happiness, but it gives you much more freedom to grow in other ways. That being the case, it is important that *financial independence* be part of the specifications for your financial structure. The primary building materials for financial independence are savings and investments.

Saving and the Magic of Compounding. Saving is like a stubborn donkey. It can carry you to financial independence, but it takes discipline. Compounding provides a magic carpet that augments the plodding of the saving donkey. Compounding is simply the reinvestment of interest earned so that that money can also begin earning interest. In table 3.1, note the growth

Table 3.1

Growth of Savings through Compounding
of Interest for 15-Year Accumulation, Compounded Monthly

Monthly Savings	Interest Rate	
	8%	12%
$200	$69,207	$99,916
$500	$173,019	$249,790

realized from interest on savings compounded monthly at the two different rates of 8 percent and 12 percent. Also shown are two different amounts of monthly savings—two hundred dollars and five hundred dollars. Numbers under the interest rates are fifteen-year accumulations. And, of course, if you double these savings, the resulting accumulation doubles. Compounding is especially powerful where the interest accumulated is tax free, as in deferred annuities which I will talk about later.

If you struggled through the truth and consequences of the last chapter, you know how much you need to save to meet your objectives. I have assumed that you will continue to store up funds in your employer savings plans at your present, or higher, rate.

Allocating Your Resources. You may have determined that your savings within your employer's program alone will transport you to a carefree retirement. In that case, your primary concern will be whether you're in the right investments to maximize your return within an acceptable degree of risk. In most employer plans, the employee has some discretion in the selection of investments for his plan contributions. If you have the option to move assets to different investments within the plan, you should be alert to possible changes that would enhance your long run return.

If you plan to save outside your employer's program, keep in

Table 3.2

Suggested Allocation of Assets among Selected Investments

Allocation in Percentages

| | Age | | |
Investment	40s	50s	60s
Liquidity (savings, checking accounts, and money-market funds)	5–10%	5–10%	5–10%
Current income (bonds, low leverage real estate)**	10–15%	15–20%	20–30%
Deferred annuities*	0	0–10% *	15–20%
Growth (common stocks, leveraged real estate)**	70–90%	50–60%	25–40%
Purchasing power hedge (precious metals, coins)	10–15%	10–15%	5–10%

*A deferred annuity is a strong candidate for investment after about age 55.

**If you don't want to manage real estate, you should consider more stocks, a mutual fund that invests in Government National Mortage Association Obligations (GNMAs), well-backed second deeds of trust, or real estate partnerships.

mind that diversification is advisable. Regardless of where or how you save, the money saved must be allocated to an appropriate mix of investments. One suggested distribution is shown in table 3.2. There's nothing absolute about this allocation. It gives you a starting point from which you might want to deviate some, depending on your circumstances and temperament.

Suppose you have reached the age of fifty without an employer savings plan and have saved very little other money. If you're serious about financial independence, you have your work cut out for you. Figure 2.1 of chapter 2 tells that story, too. If you find it very difficult to make the projections to arrive at the bottom line, you can at least get started with your savings by using a rule of thumb used by some financial advisors. Assuming you have at least ten years to go to retirement, saving 15 or 20 percent of your income each month will give you a nice nest egg. But you may eventually be eating dog food if you don't have a pension to go with it.

Risk and Reward. The essence of successful investment is to find the best possible answer to the question, "How can I earn the most on my assets with the least possible risk?" Since every investment has some kind of risk, and there are several kinds and levels of risk, selecting the best investments is a continuous trade-off between return and risk.

My friend Earl just turned fifty-five. At his birthday party, he and I retreated to a quiet corner to talk about retirement.

"You know," he began, "I used to be a wild-eyed speculator. I had the gambler's attitude that if I just took enough chances I would someday hit it big. I made some money and lost some, lucky to break even. When it finally seeped through my thick skull that I was going to be fifty-five years old, I decided to swear off the high risk investments. It suddenly dawned on me that if I speculate at this age, I'm actually taking more risk than if I were thirty. I want to retire in five years. I don't have time anymore to make up for serious mistakes."

Earl is right. As you get closer to retirement, you should lean more and more toward conserving your capital. Invest for income and moderate growth—moderate to low risk. I never look at high-risk investments anymore.

Table 3.3 is a handy comparison of risk in some of the more common investments, and it also gives you some idea of their comparative future appreciation and liquidity.

Don't reach for unusually high returns on your money. With very few exceptions, the higher the return, the higher the risk. And the various investments carry different types of risk. A good planner or broker can explain what they are for any particular investment. Or you can find out yourself through reading.[1]

I recommend that between the ages of fifty and sixty-five, if

Table 3.3
Investments—Type vs. Objectives

Investment Type	Safety of Principal in Constant Dollars	Future Appreciation*	Liquidity
Money market investments, T-bills, money market funds and accounts	Good to excellent	Generally none	Very good
Common stocks			
Income stocks	Fair	Some	Good
Growth stocks	Moderate to poor	Moderate to great	Good
Bonds (high quality corporate and government issues)	Good to excellent	Generally none except discounted bonds	Good
Mutual funds (common stocks)	Fair to poor	Moderate to great	Good
Real estate (income producing, other than residence)	Generally good	Moderate to great	Relatively poor
Deferred annuities	Excellent	None— interest only	Good after penalty phase**
Precious metals (gold, silver)	Fair to poor	Low to great	Good

*In general, the hedge against inflation follows quite closely the data on future appreciation.

**The annuity company usually has a diminishing penalty over the first five to eight years. Also if money is withdrawn before age 59 1/2, there is a government penalty as well as taxes due.

you have any high-risk investments, you gradually move most of these assets into moderate to low-risk investments. "But," you protest, "I have been very successful investing in high-risk speculations. If I'm satisfied with my results, why change?" You may have a point. However, as you approach the retirement goal line, you and your financial advisor should go into a huddle to decide whether to kick a low-risk/fewer-points field goal or go for the higher-risk/more-points touchdown. If you go for the high-risk/high-reward and lose, how will you feel? Can you live with the loss? Is it worth the risk to go for greater return?

MANAGING YOUR INVESTMENTS

We all make mistakes; it's an inevitable part of life. And when I think of some of the not-so-smart things I've done (particularly in investment management), I am reminded of the old English proverb, "Stupidity won't kill you, but it can sure make you sweat."

Due to changing circumstances, carelessness, or whatever, investment management is not an exact science, and investors and their advisors don't claim infallibility. Therefore, mistakes are bound to happen. But there are two techniques that will minimize mistakes: (1) investigating potential investments thoroughly before committing funds (don't act on hot tips) and (2) diversifying your investments.

Now before we discuss some of the possible investments, let's review important factors in making an investment decision. Frequently I hear people say, "I want the highest return I can get for the risk I am willing to take." Translated, this means that their concerns are:

▶ Safety of principal
▶ Hedge against inflation

▸ Future income
▸ Current income
▸ Liquidity of the investment
▸ Marketability of the investment
▸ Ease of management

Quite clearly, not all of these desirable traits in optimum degree will be found in any one investment. Therefore, investing becomes a matter of diversification and trade-offs to get the best combination for the individual investor. Review again tables 3.2 and 3.3.

Tax Shelters. With the passage of the Tax Reform Act of 1986, most exotic tax shelters have gone the way of the dinosaurs. Retroactive and phase-in provisions are causing sleepless nights for some people who invested in deep tax shelters. Many new investment products are now stressing income rather than sheltering. This approach changes the way such investments are evaluated. Obviously, they should be compared with other income-producing investments.

The exotic shelters may be gone, but there are still shelters. Operating your own business is one. You can have a tax-deferring Keogh plan for a significant portion of your earnings. If you establish such a plan, it is then up to you to decide what to invest the money in.

IRAs still exist, but new limitations make them less attractive. As with Keogh plans, you must decide what investments to put the IRA money into. Tax-sheltered annuities (TSAs) are still available for persons who work for certain nonprofit employers such as public education systems. There remain, of course, some tax advantages in many other investments such as real estate, but they will be considered incidental to the discussion of those investments.

As a basic rule, don't invest in anything simply for tax advantages. Select investments that are economically sound but those that minimize your tax exposure and increase in value more rapidly than inflation.

Annuities. There are several ways of classifying annuities, and for our purposes we will classify them in two types based on when benefit payments begin—(1) immediate annuities and (2) deferred annuities.

The immediate annuity is one in which you give a lump-sum premium to an insurance company and they immediately begin to pay you a monthly income for life, or for a fixed term specified in the contract. Part of this monthly payment is a return of your original premium, so you never see that money again except as it comes to you in these payments over time.

The single premium deferred annuity is one in which you again give a lump-sum premium to an insurance company, but the payments to you are deferred till a later time. In the meantime, the money you have given the insurance company accumulates earnings on which taxes are deferred until you begin to draw money from the annuity. With this type, you have a choice. At the end of the deferred period, you either withdraw the money, pay taxes on the earnings, and invest in something else; or you "annuitize." If you choose to annuitize, your original premium plus accumulated earnings become an immediate annuity. An income for life or for a fixed period as you choose.

Two advantages of annuities are safety and ease of management. These attributes are especially attractive to single women. Annuities can provide a high, secure cash flow if you're old enough. But if you buy an immediate annuity before age sixty-five or seventy, you will get a low return on your money relative to other investments. That's because of the longer pay-out period if you are younger.

Between ages fifty and sixty-five, the single premium deferred annuity can be a very good investment, especially if you need diversification and safety. Besides high safety, it provides tax-deferred accumulation of earnings at competitive rates. The combined power of compounding and tax deferral is particularly impressive.

Features of these annuities vary with the insurance company. Shop around and compare features such as current interest rate, minimum guaranteed rate, death benefit, penalty for early withdrawal, loan provisions, and amount you can withdraw penalty-free during the deferred period.

Real Estate. For many people, the best investment they will ever make may be a home. In some areas, single family houses have appreciated more with less risk than any other investment. If yours is appreciating and your neighborhood is not deteriorating, it will probably continue to be a good investment helping you to keep up with future inflation.

As you approach retirement, one of the decisions you will face is whether or not to move. And if you decide to move what should you do with the house? Should you keep the house for a rental or sell it? Of course, there are many factors that will affect that decision. But here we will consider only the investment merit of rental housing.

Under the right conditions, income property has been, and will continue to be, a good investment. But complying with the conditions of the new tax law is a sticky wicket. It is necessary for you to actively manage your property to reap all the tax benefits. If you are unwilling to do that, you can look for alternative investments. But remember that personally managed income property gets more favorable tax treatment than most alternatives.

Although they no longer provide the attractive tax shelter they once did, real estate partnerships are another possible option if you don't want to manage your own properties. But they should be investigated thoroughly. Find a disinterested person with the expertise, perhaps your investment advisor, who can do a cash-flow analysis to determine the merits of a prospective investment.

Stocks. Investors buy stocks for either income or capital growth or both. When carefully selected, stocks have done well by their investors. Generally, I advocate investing for the long term, but there are times to buy and times to sell. Some who are good at it do considerable trading. For the average person, it is usually better to only go with the big swings. The usual ways to invest are:

▶ Select your own individual stocks, deciding when to buy and sell. Use a good source of information such as *Value Line Investment Guide,* available by that name in most libraries. Or you can subscribe to the service.

▶ Invest in no-load (no-sales-fee) mutual funds, selecting your own based on your own research. *Forbes* magazine periodically has a good mutual fund evaluation.

▶ Buy and sell, i.e., trading, whether individual stocks or mutual funds, based on consultation with an investment advisor.

Fixed Income Securities. We will only consider a limited number of the infinite variety of fixed income investments. Bonds are the most common, and there are many types of them.

The price of a bond is directly related to the interest called for in the bond (the coupon rate) and the market interest rate. The coupon rate normally remains fixed throughout the life of the bond. Market interest rates will vary. As the market rate goes up, the market value (price) of the bond goes down. Because of the relationship between the price of a bond and these interest rates, bonds are a better buy when market interest rates are high than when they are low. However, the relative safety of high-grade industrial bonds and government bonds is worth something. For that reason, they may have a place in your portfolio, when you want good current safe income.

At its maturity date, a bond's market value is the same as the face value appearing on the bond. Therefore, you can prevent loss of principal by buying bonds with maturity dates no later than the date that you will want to cash them in. You can avoid the headache of having to make a selection if you buy a bond mutual fund. But one disadvantage of a bond mutual fund is that you can't select the bonds or their maturity dates.

Depending on your tax bracket, you may want to consider tax-free municipal bonds. For this purpose, I recommend buying municipal bond mutual funds, rather than individual bonds, to give you diversification and better liquidity. But they have the same disadvantage of other bond mutual funds. You can't select the bonds or their maturity dates.

Another way to enjoy a relatively high current return is to buy into a securities fund that invests in Government National Mortgage Association Obligations (GNMAs). Their portfolio consists primarily of mortgages guaranteed by the federal government.

SPENDING IT WISELY

A gray-haired couple was seen in a big new Cadillac with a sign in the back window, "Being of sound mind, we spent it all." We all know that a fool and his money are soon parted. But since we can't take a U-haul trailer with us when we leave this life, the philosophy of the Cadillac-owning couple just might have some merit.

Now before you can go on a spending binge, be it wise or not, there is one very important necessity—money. The money you have set aside for retirement does not appear in your hands until you have decided on the method of payout and signed your name on some papers. This is true for your pension as well as your savings plans. Depending on what savings plan you have had (a company-sponsored, tax-deferred 401(k) or IRAs or Keogh or some other) there are several options open to you. Two examples of these options are rollovers into IRAs or tax-deferred annuities or a lump sum distribution with five-year forward averaging.

Regardless, Uncle Sam will be there looking over your shoulder, and how much he can take depends on the options you choose and your circumstances. Before you make your decisions, be sure to consult a first-rate tax expert, and you will end up with more money to indulge your spending whims.

Spending wisely is an integral part of good money management. Obviously, you want to provide well for your spouse and family. And certainly a reasonable quality of life that includes vacations is in order. But what you choose to spend on these things is entirely a personal matter. Beyond that, if you are still blessed with a surplus, giving some of it away could greatly help other people and give you much satisfaction.

For example, I know of one multi-millionaire couple who have decided to give their four children the finest of educations; beyond that, they plan to leave each one only $20,000. Their reasoning is that the children won't need the money and that too much might destroy their incentive to be all that they can be. The bulk of their estate will be given to their church and charities.

A rather common practice among seniors and retirees is to help their children with something specific like buying a home. Fred and Eleanor did this with their son and daughter-in-law on a strictly business basis just as they would have done with any other partners. Each couple became a half-owner paying one half of everything: down payment, mortgage payments, taxes, etc. And to be able to treat it as a rental for tax purposes, Fred and Eleanor had to charge the kids one-half of a fair monthly rent for the half that Fred and Eleanor owned. Being very responsible, the kids enthusiastically performed their part of the bargain and three years later bought out their parents half interest. Both couples gained through this deal. But be sure to keep all such deals on a strictly business basis.

There are many wise ways to help your own children. And it makes more sense to help them while you're still alive than to leave an inheritance that they can fight over. When you have several children, care must be taken to keep things equitable.

Neither of these examples should necessarily be adopted as a blueprint for you. They are merely intended to stimulate your thinking. There are so many things that can be done with even modest means. With some brainstorming you should be able to reveal some exciting possibilities. And in your thinking and planning consider this. Happiness does not consist of the blind pursuit of more and more material things. Enough is enough. Good management of money is a virtue. Worshiping it is not.

CHAPTER FOUR

TRAINING FOR THE VINTAGE YEARS

They called him "Lucky Lindy." It was a name he hated, but he could do nothing to purge it from the media. Those privileged to view the episode from behind the scenes knew it was not a matter of luck.

Oh yes, the time was ripe. Circumstances seemed to be poised on the brink of a great achievement. But Charles A. Lindbergh left nothing to chance that wasn't absolutely necessary. Meticulous planning went into both the design of the Spirit of St. Louis and Lindbergh's flight plan.

Was that all? Not by a nautical mile. Next he flight tested his new, specially designed airplane, making short flights to check out his equipment: the engine, the special fuel system, flight idiosyncrasies, landing characteristics, and load-carrying capability. Then came longer flights. Lindbergh flew the Spirit of St. Louis on a record-breaking, nonstop flight east from San Diego to St. Louis and, the very next day, a second, record-breaking flight from St. Louis to New York.[1]

For publicity? No, that was incidental. He had to know how he and the airplane would perform before undertaking the ultimate test—the first solo, nonstop, trans-Atlantic flight by a heavier-than-air craft.

Planning and practice did not guarantee Lindbergh's successful flight across the Atlantic, but they greatly increased his chances of avoiding a crash. The same is true for successful retirement. Careful planning and practice can make the difference between dreams that soar into reality and those that crash.

WINDOW SHOPPING: SAMPLING THE GOODIES

Our primary emphasis thus far has been on retirement planning. Although planning is important, it is only one phase of your preparation for the big change that retirement brings. The plan is your guide—where you want to go and what you need to do to get there. But you may have the best flight plan in the world and still not be prepared to fly the airplane. Just as Lindbergh built his confidence through hours of flight testing, you, too, can benefit from pre-retirement training, or practicing. Whatever you call it, it is primarily implementing your plan. It consists of finding answers to your questions and working out the action items. In general terms, it means doing what you need to do to reach your goals.

Sound formidable? It won't once you find out how much fun it is.

You might call it window shopping. What better way to find out what retirement possibilities appeal to you. When you spot some things that attract you (like Danish pastry in a bakery window), sample them. If you think that traveling in a motor home is close to paradise, rent one and try it. Maybe you picture yourself as a photographer. Why not take a course in photography at a local community college? That's the way to take a bite of retirement and savor the flavor. If you don't like the taste of that bite, try another.

The interests you choose are an entirely personal matter. You can pick and choose interests solely on the basis of what you enjoy the most, first priority being assigned to those that fit your criteria of what is important to you and what makes life worth living. But how do you know for sure what you will enjoy the most? Unless you have a one-track mind, you won't. That's exactly the point. You need to try some things to find out what you will really enjoy the most, such as where you will live and what you will do. Take time to explore those long-suppressed interests and unused talents. For example, perhaps:

▶ You would like to pursue an old hobby or try a new one.

▶ Your woodworking tools are rusting in the garage.

▶ Photography or painting appeals to you.

▶ You look forward to reading certain great books.

▶ You know you could knock ten strokes off your golf game if you just did more golfing.

▶ There are so many places in the world you have dreamed about visiting.

▶ You have a great idea for a small business.

▶ Part-time income from a staff position in your present company appeals to you.

▶ A friend asked you to contribute your considerable talent to a very worthy volunteer project.

▶ You just know that living in the town of Smooth Sailing in the state of Bliss would be simply that.

▶ On the other hand, your spouse thinks that a year of motorhome traveling to see the country would be ecstasy.

Before retirement, list some of these brilliant and appealing ideas in the order of their appeal to you now. Then try them. You will discover some interesting things about yourself. Some of the things that you thought were most attractive to you will turn out not to be. There may be some exciting surprises. And think of the time you have saved when once you retire. If you know what you want, your transition will be as smooth as peeled onions. Just remember, the operative words in this flurry of activity are, "before retirement."

HOW TO FIND SOURCES OF HELP

When I was a college freshman, I had a delightful chemistry professor. Any time he felt philosophical, we could tell by the smile on his face that he was about to wax eloquent with some of his homespun wisdom. And hidden somewhere therein would be his favorite saying, "You can learn something from everyone you meet."

Professor Anderson believed there was more to life than chemistry. My brain agreed, but my eighteen-year-old hormones were not so sure. Of course, they were urged on by a different chemistry. Furthermore, I had other things on my mind—like passing my calculus and chemistry exams, wondering who was going to win our next football game, and scrounging enough money to take my date to a movie. At the time these seemed more important than Professor Anderson's philosophy. It was not until I had struggled through some ten years of war and peace, meeting many people in the process, that I realized the profundity of what Professor Anderson had said.

He was right. And that wisdom applies to retirement preparation. *Retirees and about-to-retirees can be a great source of know-how in the fine art of retirement.* Rarely do they do everything in the best possible way, but right or wrong, they are blessed with 20-20 hindsight. They will, of course, be looking in the rear-view mirror from their own particular vantage point. But I think you will be pleasantly surprised at how helpful their input can be. Not only that, but asking their advice is a great way to bring joy into the lives of some older people. In fact, you might even find that it will give them a visible lift and you'll see a new sparkle in their eyes. So engage them in dialogue, really listen, and you will benefit from their perspective. If you gain their confidence, they are often quite candid. And why not. They have nothing to lose. And they see it as an opportunity to use their experience to benefit someone else—another reason for living.

Before my own retirement, I talked to dozens of retirees and people that were thinking about retirement or actively planning it. In these many conversations one of the themes I heard espoused over and over again was the one I have emphasized in this book. Try things before retirement.

I realize that, due to circumstances, you may have to try some things after retirement. The objective is to try everything you can (you be the judge) before retirement.

Other sources of help for your retirement planning are seminars, which have proliferated over the past few years. Many companies now give seminars to employees they consider to be in that you-should-be-planning-your-retirement age group. But there are also many seminars given by independent individuals and organizations. Although most of these seminars concentrate exclusively on financial matters, they usually do a credible job in their area of expertise. But with some, their main goal is to sell their products. Always check these with some professional you can trust before you get sucked into a bad deal.

The hundreds of senior centers across the country are another source of help. These centers are excellent sources of information about retirement, and you don't have to be a senior citizen to use them. Start now talking, listening, observing, gathering information, and finally practicing.

FIRST LAW OF SUCCESSFUL RETIREMENT

Brenda did it right. When she retired, she wanted a change of scene. Not just a move around the corner, but clear across the country from New Jersey to California. She leased the house she owned in New Jersey, traveled to California, and rented a house there. She plans to stay a year before she pulls up her New Jersey roots. By that time, she will have lived through a full year of season changes, explored cultural opportunities, made some friends, and absorbed impressions of other things California has to offer.

By the end of the year, Brenda will have savored the flavor of life in her adopted state. If at that time the taste is not to her liking, she can easily return to her former location wiser for her experience and with scarcely a smidgen of inconvenience.

Brenda is following "the first law of successful retirement (which is, by chance, the same as the first law of wing walking): 'Never leave hold of what you've got until you've got hold of something else.'"[2]

So simple. And yet I know of several other people who failed to follow the law and got mangled between a rock and a hard place. This first-law wisdom applies equally well to most of the other changes you may consider when approaching the next passage in your life.

» Glen and Darlene «

When I first met Glen, he was a civil engineer with an artistic temperament. Although the painting displayed in his den testified to his talent with paint and canvas, Glen had pursued a career as an engineer in an architectural firm. With a wife and four children, much of his salary went to put food on the table and a roof over their heads. But Glen was dazzled with a vision of riches in real estate. So for twenty-one years Glen and Darlene plowed their savings into real estate in Northern California. Then Glen began building the foundation for a sideline.

He waded through real estate courses and exams to get a real estate salesman's license. Further classes and experience earned him a broker's license. To that he added an insurance salesman's license.

Four years later, business in the architectural firm shriveled, and he was asked to accept a salary reduction. After he and

Darlene assessed their resources, they decided that he could bail out and strike out on his own. But they were both worried about making such a major change so late in Glen's career life. He was 54 years old. Would this destroy their chance for a secure retirement in case their new venture didn't work out as they planned?

The first two years were touch and go. Children in college drained their savings, and a real estate slump almost capsized his new career before it left the dock.

But before his ship sank, he was rescued by a fortunate business turnaround. From there it has been mostly smooth sailing in a fair breeze. With sales and investments, Glen has constructed a golden galleon for his retirement.

Glen says of his success, "I worked hard, but I was very lucky, too. I have always believed in being prepared, but I had no idea what I was preparing for."

» Sam and Jean «

Shaped like a welterweight boxer, short and muscular, Sam is both competitive and pugnacious. His academic credentials include an M.B.A. degree with a strong emphasis in mathematics. Before retiring, he was a contracts supervisor in a small firm.

Sam's lifetime hobby has been woodworking, particularly furniture making. When I walked into his garage, I found him leaning over his whirling jointer. Hands pale with sawdust, he finished running the board through the machine and switched it off. I soon learned that Sam attacks a woodworking project with unreserved energy, enjoying it to the full. The need for a sense of closure that he developed in his former job demands rapid progress toward the completion of any project. But he is always ready to take a break and discuss his latest endeavor, which on this occasion came as quite a surprise.

"Guess what," he said. "That teaching credential I got three years before I retired is beginning to pay off. And I don't mean in money. I'm having a great time. The high school down the street needed a mathematics instructor. I applied and got the job. Been teaching three classes a week. Those kids are fun, and I feel useful. Didn't know I could relate to high school kids like that. It's exciting."

Later over coffee, Jean confided, "Before he got this teaching job, Sam was driving me into a case of high blood pressure. He has so much energy, I thought he was going to blow a gasket. And he had lost his feeling of self-worth. Things have been different since he started teaching."

Sam now has two pieces of the retirement pie: a hobby he loves and an exciting contribution to the younger generation. And it's all because of action he took before retirement.

PRACTICING FOR OTHER ADVENTURES

If you have window-shopped for retirement occupations (anything on which you might choose to spend time), no doubt, you have some ideas churning around in your head—perhaps so many it is confusing. I should emphasize that the term occupation as I use it here can mean any absorbing activity—paid or unpaid work, volunteer activities, a hobby, or sport.

In case the concept of "practicing for retirement" is still somewhat unclear to you, consider the following words from the book *Learn to Grow Old* by Dr. Paul Tournier:

> Success in any undertaking always demands some training, the establishment of reflexes and habits, and some ability, if not a proper apprenticeship, and these things do not come easily at a more advanced age if they have not been started earlier. . . . success in retirement depends in great measure on the way we have lived beforehand.[3]

Let the significance of those words penetrate your mind. ". . . *success in retirement depends in great measure on the way we have lived beforehand.*" In other words, we can blow our retirement before we even get there.

Research among retired people has demonstrated that there is a certain necessary continuity in life. Most people, when they reach retirement age, tend to continue in the direction they were moving at the time of retirement. They act the same way, harbor the same attitudes, have the same values, and do the same things one year after retirement as they did one day before retirement. As I see it, it's a phenomenon of human nature with an aging factor thrown in. But because of this tendency on the part of us humans, it is rare for a retired person who has had no other occupation than his work to take up an entirely new activity. It might be easier to teach your dog to talk.

Those who have done other things during their working lives are likely to fall back on something they have done before, or try something new for a while and then give up. The retiree who has no previous activity to fall back on is often lost.

However, starting something new after retirement and succeeding at it is not impossible. With the old "can-do spirit" anything is possible. But it's almost like being born again, in a non-theological sense. Tournier is saying that it is rare for a person to succeed under those circumstances. Let's face it. When an older person tries something new, he or she is behind the statistical eight-ball.

It is a fact of life that the best way to improve your odds for a successful transition into retirement is to begin a potential retirement occupation years ahead of time. It matters not whether it is part-time or full-time paid employment, volunteer work, or an engrossing hobby or sport. Just do it.

In *Learn to Grow Old*, Dr. Tournier also has a great deal to say about hobbies and spare-time occupations. For one thing, they are not necessarily the answer for every retiree who wants a meaningful way to spend time. Some hobbies may be great as a change of pace from a primary vocation, but if they are the only things left with which to fill life after retirement, they may soon lose much of their attraction. Then boredom replaces pleasure.

To be adequate for the retiree, an occupation that began as a hobby or spare-time activity during employment must be able to provide the retiree with a sense of purpose in life. It must be an absorbing interest. So do not just assume that your hobbies will fill the bill. They didn't do it for me. To put that smile of fulfillment on your face, what you choose to do must have significance to you—not necessarily to anyone else, just you. If, in your view, your activity is important and makes life worthwhile, you are home free. The more engrossed and enthusiastic you are with it, the better. But start the ball rolling before you retire.

NETWORKING WITH FRIENDS

Finding something to retire to should not be a solo flight. Others can help with the navigation, guiding you around thunderstorms and through the fog. That, among other things, is what friends are for.

When I retired, I was sure I had thought of everything. I had often dreamed of pursuing a variety of outside interests, most of which I had little time for before retirement. In planning my retirement, it seemed that all I had to do was dust off those tantalizing ideas and have at it. But it was nowhere near that simple.

My wife, Alice, and I enjoyed good health. We had planned adequately for our financial needs, but the psychological aspects bewildered me. Alice was a teacher and retired two years before I did. She slipped into retirement as smoothly and decisively as Jack Nicklaus swings a golf club. She knew exactly what she wanted to do and proceeded to do it. Consequently, she could not understand why my retirement transition was like giving birth to a litter of hippos.

The problem was that I had not asked and answered the right questions. Instead, I tried to solo. So I floundered from peak to valley, alternately happy and depressed and everything in between. I was busy but not satisfied. I needed something else—a sense of direction, an absorbing interest that I could feel was important. After wallowing in this swamp of frustration for about two years, I finally managed to slosh my way to more solid ground. Subsequently, I realized I had allowed myself to be programmed by well-worn, strident slogans and flag-waving declarations of personal independence.

What I'm getting at is this. We have been taught to be strong, to stand on our own two feet, to acknowledge and solve our own problems. All of which will carry us just so far. But what I came to see is that in a situation like retirement transition, we need to ask friends for help. I now belong to a support group which happens to be a group of men from our church who meet for breakfast once a week. (There are also groups of women.) Topics of conversation range from jobs to computers to personal concerns. Nothing is off limits. And I have many other friends who, I understand now, could have helped unhook me from the horns of my dilemma.

Broadcast experimental signals which tell people you are willing to try some things. And when you come up with ideas, remember that your friends can help make them work, and be happy to do it.

Then when opportunity knocks and they offer a solution you like, open the door. But to keep friendships from coming unraveled, be up front with your acceptance. (They may have an agreement that either party to the deal can cut it off, in case they don't like it, with no hard feelings.)

LANDING SAFELY FROM A BAD JUMP

An energetic, delightful couple, exciting to be around—that's Andy and Joanne. Their attitudes and enthusiasm are contagious. As I talked with them, it was obvious that their retirement experience had been both stimulating and fulfilling, even though it had gotten off to a shaky start.

Joanne is a retired elementary school teacher; she retired a few years before her husband, who continued to hold a teaching position in a community college. Andy had started his retirement planning and intended to work a few more years when suddenly he was confronted with a health problem which made an earlier retirement mandatory. Mixed emotions, mostly negative, flooded his mind. He was scared. He felt that he was hurtling toward retirement in a free fall. Fortunately, his parachute opened just in time.

Andy talked to friends about his plans to retire early. When the word got around, he and Joanne were offered an opportunity they couldn't refuse (a happy example of what talking with people can do for you).

All their working life, Andy and Joanne had traveled a lot. That interest in travel, cultivated over the years, unwittingly prepared them for the new opportunity. They were invited to perform public relations work for a Christian organization that secures support for needy children in foreign countries. Except for travel expenses, they worked as unpaid volunteers and even contributed some to their own expenses.

They were as happy as two small kids slurping triple-decker ice cream cones on a hot day. Before their adventure began two and one-half months after Andy's retirement, there was just time enough for some deep breathing to fill their lungs with the refreshing air of freedom.

They began their public relations work by visiting the organization's facilities in Guatemala, Mexico, Singapore, and Hong Kong. Interspersed with these foreign trips were the lecture circuits to private Christian schools and public schools encouraging people to sponsor children in these foreign countries. For Andy, the exciting and challenging activity of the next four and one-half years was like a new short career—an opportunity to wind down from his previous full-time occupation.

This was an ideal assignment for these two retirees—they loved to travel, they were trained and experienced in speaking before groups, and they deeply believed in the cause they were promoting. Andy declares with obvious strong feelings that this experience was a great transition for which he was very thankful. In his words, "except for this activity, I would have had serious problems with my retirement."

Andy and Joanne like to switch directions frequently. The four and one-half year stint with the Christian organization was (for them) an unusually long time to continue in one direction. They have subsequently been involved in many other exciting commitments, almost all of which have been unpaid volunteer occupations.

Very active in their church, they have taken on such responsibilities as playing the organ in a convalescent hospital, working in the cafeteria in a Christian retreat center, and serving as officers in various church organizations, to name but a few. Joanne has one very interesting rule at this stage of her life. She will take on almost any responsibility, but for no longer than one year. She loves change.

With his sudden decision to retire, Andy realized his retirement preparation was flawed. He would not have adequate time before retirement to carry out his plan for developing a new occupation—something that would give him a stimulating purpose for his later years. Painfully aware of his brother's early death, he was scared. His brother had died six months after he retired because he had nothing to retire to. With no dream, no plans, no absorbing interest, and no hope, his brother had no reason for living. Today Andy believes that the timely offer of an exciting transition helped him avoid an untimely demise.

Andy and Joanne were lucky. Although Andy's retirement preparation was seriously flawed, friends rescued him from his tailspin toward an almost certain crash. The result—a happy landing.

Andy spoke with strong emotion when I asked what advice he would give other people. "Start planning early. If I had it to do over again, I would actively look for and develop a new occupation years before my planned date of retirement."

CHAPTER FIVE

ENERGIZED WITH WINNING ATTITUDES

Rare is the man who has not been suddenly jolted by wise words from his wife. Sometimes they explode like a well-directed torpedo. Other times they are so subtle that days after the confrontation a light flashes and you realize you've been had.

The other day it was torpedoes at twenty paces. In such a confrontation, I usually shoot myself in the foot. Alice seldom loses her cool, but this time her anger erupted. While I was pondering the alternatives, a sore foot or ignominious retreat, she shattered me with a direct hit.

"I'm thoroughly fed up with your grumbling and negative attitudes," she said. "You've got the world by the tail and don't know what to do with it. What if you had multiple sclerosis like our friend Jenny? Then you'd have something to grumble about."

"Jenny doesn't grumble," I said lamely.

"So, you've noticed."

Sometimes it takes a shot like that to make me think. That explosion swiveled my head 180 degrees and rattled a few brain cells. There's no doubt about it, Alice is a wise woman. She knows when to be subtle and when to fire her big guns. I concluded that indeed my attitudes had regressed to where they were about as pleasant as an infestation of fleas. And I determined to do something about it.

ATTITUDES ARE ALL-IMPORTANT

Attitudes are our customary manner of emotional response—our manner of thinking, behaving, or reacting—our mental outlook. But the important thing about attitudes is that we can choose them.

Dr. Viktor Frankl, the Jewish psychiatrist who was imprisoned by the Nazis during the Holocaust, discovered there was something that the Nazis could not take away even if they took his life—namely, the attitude with which he chose to respond to his situation. That is the one power he held over his captors; he could chose his response to them. He could choose bitterness, hatred, or self-pity or forgiveness and hope coupled with a determination to endure and survive. Dr. Frankl chose the latter.[1]

All of us have the same power to choose our attitudes. But we don't always make wise choices, and if ever consequences were inevitable it is in the realm of attitudes. With respect to one's retirement years, the attitudes adopted earlier in life will more than likely be carried over into retirement itself.

Alice and I have two longtime friends who illustrate the consequences of attitudes. Doris, a vivacious widow, lives in her own apartment in Seattle. When we picked her up to take her to lunch, she met us all decked out in a fashionable "preppy" outfit and a big happy smile. Our luncheon conversation was lively and up to date. She manages her own finances and displayed a keen positive interest and current knowledge about what was going on in the world. She exuded enthusiasm. And I'm sure it was obvious that our reaction to her was very positive.

Doris drives her own car. Her apartment is filled with her own paintings. When I asked her what she did in her spare time, she said she knitted shawls and afghans for the old people. At that time Doris was ninety-two years young—happy and optimistic, with a zest for living.

We visited Martha in a retirement home. She greeted us with a frowning face even though she said she was glad to see us. We spent the time listening to her complaints and her negative assessment of life. She has no interests, no hobbies, no sense of humor, and didn't know or care about what was going on in the world. At age seventy-two, Martha looks and is morose, cynical, grumpy, frumpy, and negative.

We have known these women for thirty-seven years. Neither Doris nor Martha have any serious health problems. When we first met them, Doris was happy, optimistic, positive, outgoing, enthusiastic, and interested in many things. Martha was unhappy, pessimistic, ingrown, self-centered, and negative.

Both women have lived through the rainstorms of life; but after the rain, Doris saw the flowers, whereas Martha saw only mud puddles. In thirty-seven years they haven't changed. The really ironical part is that during all these years Martha could have been just as happy as Doris. No person or external circumstances forced either of these women to be the way they were. It was simply their way of thinking—the way they responded to the world and their circumstances. They chose their own attitudes.

The fact is, Doris likes herself, other people, and the world in general. Martha does not. Doris has a sense of personal worth (self-esteem) and self-confidence. Martha does not. These attitudes and feelings about themselves carry over into their feelings toward other people and life in general.

If we don't feel good about ourselves most of the time, there is something wrong. To develop peace of mind, we need to be reasonably free from worry, guilt, internal conflict, fear, and envy. Yet, where these feelings exist, they are elements of our state of mind and largely reflect the attitudes which we choose.

Over the years, Doris's exuberance has attracted many friends. Recently, she told us that she has been invited to four separate dinners to celebrate her ninety-fifth birthday. These thrilling events confirm that her life is full to the brim.

Martha exudes unhappiness. But she doesn't seem to understand that her morose and negative attitudes repel people. That she has few visitors affirms her negative attitudes and returns her to unhappiness—a vicious circle. In all these years, who has been courageous enough to suggest to her that her attitudes have been shaping her destiny? Would she have listened? Would she have, as she could have, done something about it? Now the sun is setting on her empty life.

A TRANSFORMED MIND—KEY TO QUALITY LIVING

Psychologists are finding that although a person may be chronologically ready for retirement and have the desire and adequate finances to retire, he or she may not be psychologically prepared.

Researchers have found that when we must adjust to some big change in life, such as retirement, our attitudes about ourselves and our lifestyle can spell the difference between joy and frustration. Dr. David D. Burns in his book *Feeling Good: The New Mood Therapy* says the negative thoughts that flood our minds are the actual cause of our self-defeating emotions.[2] However, good attitudes do not make problems disappear, they only shrink them down to coping size.

In talking with dozens of retirees, I discovered that tuning in to their true feelings about retirement usually required more than just a casual conversation. When I asked each one how they felt about retirement, I seldom heard a discouraging word or a negative response. The answer was usually "fine, great, I'm enjoying it, or I'm happy."

Occasionally I heard something more evasive like, "don't I look like I'm happy?" In further conversation with someone who gave that kind of answer, I usually found that person was neither very happy nor unhappy. He had merely adapted himself to the monotony of the vacuum of a meaningless existence.

Is it possible to predict which persons will be happy in retirement and which ones will not?

Many researchers and writers have tried to categorize and label seniors and retirees in various ways to support statistical studies. Some have used social levels, job status categories, or income levels (high income strata and low income strata). Then they made studies to ascertain how well the various categories adjusted to retirement. The conclusions were often misleading. There were just too many influences that were unaccounted for—too many variables.

The subtleties of happiness continue to baffle the statisticians. In my opinion, the conclusion that came closest to the truth was that of Harry Hepner, emeritus professor of psychology at Syracuse University. After his research, he stated that:

> Many different interpretations of happiness and patterns of adjustment to retirement were found, but one especially successful retirement group consisted of those whose occupational status, position in the community, education, health, or recreational activity followed no special pattern. They were, however, enjoying a kind of happiness favorable to peace and wisdom; they were living in terms of a sustaining framework of thinking that gave purpose to their lives. They had facial expressions of outward calm and, more importantly, their whole manner portrayed an inner serenity, a serenity which indicated that they had learned to enjoy the gift of living. They were happy, and yet they had not sought happiness as such. Happiness came to them, as it must to all men, not as an end in itself but as a by-product or side effect. It came to them because they had somehow learned to live in terms of a continuing interest, a theme, a code of ethics, or a goal that gave a lasting feeling of self-fulfillment. They lived for something more important than the attainment of personal happiness.[3]

Most people who continue to grow in terms of education, personal and spiritual development, maturity, and higher levels of accomplishment during their working years continue this pattern by doing very meaningful things during retirement.

In other words, the pattern established by a person before retirement seems to follow that individual right on into retirement. So if you think that the mere changing of your status from employed to retired is going to make you happy, forget it. Retirement in itself will not magically transform negative attitudes into positive ones. Your chances of that happening are no better than the probability of your winning a state lottery.

The key to quality living in your later years is to transform your thinking before retirement. A healthy frame of mind will transport you a long way on the road to an exciting, fulfilling life. All the plans and preparation in the world without the mental preparation are no better than a flight plan without an airplane. You won't get off the ground.

LIVING WITH MURPHY'S LAWS

Life is not a bed of roses. Many things that happen to us are beyond our control. Some people are born with handicaps. Accidents happen. Tornadoes, earthquakes, and wars often strike people in seemingly random fashion.

But to characterize some of the more mundane, day-to-day frustrations that can make you think someone is out to get you, consider the long list of inescapable "laws" of life commonly called "Murphy's Laws." Here's a sample of these laws modified with a parochial twist.

▸ Nothing is as easy as it looks; everything takes longer than you think; if anything can go wrong it will, and at the worst possible time.

▸ The other line always moves faster.

▸ The chance of the bread falling with the peanut butter-and-jelly side down is directly proportional to the cost of the carpet.

▶ Whatever hits the fan will not be evenly distributed.

▶ The light at the end of the tunnel is the headlamp of an oncoming train.

▶ If you're feeling good, don't worry. You'll get over it.[4]

Certainly it's easy to get the impression sometimes that life has handed you a can of worms. The bad things that can happen, and often do, assault your attitudes. How can we deal with that?

RESPONDING TO LIFE WITH INVINCIBLE SPIRIT

There are two very common responses to life's problems which are totally counterproductive. One is blaming someone: ourself, some other person, God, or fate. Blaming ourselves will lay a guilt trip on us and reduce our self-esteem. If we blame God or someone else, we destroy relationships and wallow in doubt and cynicism.

The other negative response is self-pity, which in its depths might lead us to feel as Job did when he cursed the day of his birth (Job 3:1). Feeling sorry for oneself can lead to depression. Then it's not easy to think rationally. But I have found that if I can just get my brain to function partially, I can turn it over to God through prayer. As was so well said by the apostle Paul:

> Do not be anxious about anything, but in everything, by prayer and petition, with thanksgiving, present your requests to God. And the peace of God, which transcends all understanding, will guard your hearts and your minds in Christ Jesus (Phil. 4:6–7).

Alice and I have seen invincible spirit demonstrated in the Sierra Nevada mountains where we enjoy hiking the high trails. By staying overnight at a 7000 foot camp called Tuolumne Meadows before we start our strenuous hike, we acclimate ourselves to the altitude.

The high Sierra camp "loop" begins and ends at Tuolumne Meadows. This hiking trail meanders through forest and over mountains along streams and lakes at altitudes ranging from 7000 feet to over 10,000 feet. It is seven to ten arduous miles between each of six camps.

One evening before we started our hike, we ate dinner in the camp restaurant with a group of hikers that had just completed the "loop" in seven days. Not so remarkable except that the ages of these men and women ranged from sixty-five to seventy-five years. Eyes shimmering with delight and wonder, one man who, incidentally, had emphysema kept repeating, "I did it, I did it." With such an attitude of fortitude, the human spirit can be indomitable.

I sometimes play golf at a short nine-hole course which happens to be convenient to our home. Because it is a short, easy course it is patronized mostly by older people, a few neophytes, and people with limited time.

One morning I watched an older golfer struggle to get out of his car. He shuffled around to the trunk by holding on to the car. With the help of his buddy, he lifted out his golf bag and handcart. Then, using the cart as a sort of walker, he hobbled toward the club house.

I couldn't believe this man intended to play a round of golf. When it was his turn to tee off, he managed to balance himself, wrap his gnarled hands around the club and swing. The ball soared right down the fairway. What spirit!

I've seen that same indomitable spirit in others, too.

Dana skis with one artificial leg.

Jeff and his fellow basketball players shoot baskets from wheelchairs.

Jerry, who lost his wife to cancer, spends his spare time helping and comforting those who are seriously ill or who have experienced the loss of a loved one.

I have nothing but admiration for people like that. I have seen people with arthritis, poor eyes, weak muscles, and other assorted disabilities do astounding things. They could curl up in front of a television set and feel sorry for themselves. Instead they have chosen better alternatives.

MENDING MUDDLED MOODS AND MIXED EMOTIONS

Attitudes, moods, and emotions fit together as pieces of the same human behavior puzzle. Depression, sometimes called the world's number one public health problem, can kill you. But there are many mood and emotional disorders which, though minor by comparison, can dash a person's happiness and relationships.

Dr. David D. Burns, working with a group of psychiatrists and psychologists at the University of Pennsylvania School of Medicine, has written a book called *Feeling Good: The New Mood Therapy*. This book describes a significant breakthrough in the treatment and prevention of mood disorders. Originating from the innovative work of Dr. Aaron T. Beck, this new concept is called "cognitive therapy."

Simply stated, the idea is that your thinking patterns profoundly influence your moods and emotions.

Dr. Burns asserts that a person can overcome depression and other mood disorders by learning some simple methods for mood elevation—techniques that straighten out twisted thinking. This system advocates a great deal of self-help but it is not just another pop psychology. It is based on rigorous scientific research under the critical examination of professionals in the field.

In describing this psychology, Dr. Burns says:

> The first principle of cognitive therapy is that all your moods are created by your "cognitions" or thoughts. A cognition refers to the way you look at things—your perceptions, mental attitudes, and beliefs. . . . You feel the way you do right now because of the thoughts you are thinking at this moment.

. . . The moment you have a certain thought and believe it, you will experience an immediate emotional response. Your thought actually creates the emotion.[5]

In other words, *your feelings are a mirror of the way you are thinking.* You can get a little idea of how this works in the case of dreams.

When my friend Elmer went camping with his family, he liked to sleep in a hammock stretched between two trees, while the rest of the family slept on air mattresses on the ground.

Last year they camped along the Tuolumne River near Yosemite National Park. The teen-age kids were quite excited about the bears they had seen that day. In the evening around the campfire, they got into a lively discussion about bears and whether they were a threat to the campers. The ranger assured them that if they took certain precautions to keep their food out of the bears' reach, they would be perfectly safe.

The kids' imaginations ran wild the rest of the evening trying to out-scare each other with incredible yarns about bears chasing people. Then they all went to bed with a question on their minds. What would it be like to get up in the middle of the night and come face to jowl with a bear?

As usual, Elmer unrolled his sleeping bag in his hammock, climbed in, and was soon sound asleep. The next thing he remembers is that he was being chased by a giant black bear. He managed to scramble up a small tree just out of reach of the huge jaws as the bear stood on his hind legs and shook the tree. "I began to tremble and sweat," says Elmer. "I have never been so scared. My heart pounded into overdrive as I felt myself slipping, slipping. I grabbed for a branch just out of reach, then felt myself falling. Thump."

Elmer woke up to find himself on the ground, having fallen out of the hammock. There was no bear. It had all been a dream. But it took an hour before he calmed down enough to climb back into his hammock and go to sleep. Needless to say, his wife and kids have never stopped kidding him about it.

All of this is to say, a faulty perception of the mind, whether awake or sleeping, can produce great emotional stress.

The second principle of cognitive therapy is that *feelings of depression derive from negative thoughts;* gloom pervades your perceptions of yourself and the world. Thus when you are morose, cynical, and pessimistic you may be on the brink of serious depression. With continuing repetition, you may come to believe that things really are as bad as you, in your imagination, perceive them to be.

The third principle is that the *negative thoughts which churn up your emotions nearly always contain great distortions, even though they appear valid.* Depression, for example, is based not on accurate perceptions of reality but on irrational or distorted thinking, like viewing a scene through an imperfect window or one reflected in a trick mirror.[6]

In his book, Dr. Burns explains in detail the techniques of cognitive therapy and their practical application. He helps readers to understand their moods, to cope with the stress of daily living, and discover and eliminate the mental distortions that result in painful emotions. People play an active role in their own treatment. But Dr. Burns points out that severe disturbances still need professional help.

According to Dr. Burns, the principles and techniques are relatively simple. Once learned and applied, they enable a person to control undesirable mood swings and self-destructive behavior. And as a bonus, they promote self-esteem and personal growth. But these methods do not guarantee unending joy any more than good physical conditioning will guarantee that a person will never get tired. Low points will still threaten. However, when people are deeply involved in their own treatment, the precepts of cognitive therapy become a way of living, which helps pull them through the bad times.

Results with numerous patients have proved the effectiveness of cognitive therapy. Many patients report feeling the happiest they have ever felt in their lives. With practice, they can view themselves, other people, and the world in general with the same attitudes Doris had: positive, optimistic, outgoing, and full of zest for living.

Perhaps even more remarkable than the effectiveness of this therapy is the fact that the basic idea is not new. For centuries, writers have told us about the connection between our minds and our feelings. Almost two thousand years ago, this was a hot topic with the apostle Paul. Among his writings we find these thoughts:

Do not conform any longer to the pattern of this world, but be transformed by the renewing of your mind. Then you will be able to test and approve what God's will is—his good, pleasing and perfect will (Rom. 12:2).

In another of his letters, Paul entreats the people to pray to God and then says:

Finally brothers, whatever is true, whatever is noble, whatever is right, whatever is pure, whatever is lovely, whatever is admirable—if anything is excellent or praiseworthy—think about such things (Phil. 4:8).

Paul implies that praying and thinking about the positive and good can change our attitudes and feelings. But it's not always easy to make our minds do what we want them to do, such as dwelling on desirable thoughts. So for those who feel that their attitudes, moods, and emotions could use a little touch-up, here are a few tips.

HOW TO DEVELOP WINNING ATTITUDES

Look around you. Who are the people you enjoy being with the most? What are their feelings and attitudes? Do they enjoy life?

Do they have a sense of humor? Are they optimistic, enthusiastic, and vital? Do they really savor life?

In his book *Strengthening Your Grip,* Chuck Swindoll grips the significance of attitudes in this powerful statement:

> . . . I believe the single most significant decision I can make on a day-to-day basis is my choice of attitude. It is more important than my past, my education, my bankroll, my successes or failures, fame or pain, what other people think of me or say about me, my circumstances, or my position. Attitude . . . keeps me going or cripples my progress. It alone fuels my fire or assaults my hope. When my attitudes are right, there's no barrier too high, no valley too deep, no dream too extreme, no challenge too great for me.[7]

Positive, optimistic, joyful attitudes can overcome or mitigate many deficiencies in your retirement scenario.

To acquire good attitudes, we must have a strong desire, which implies that we feel a need to change. Then we must choose to do something about it. The actual change must come from within ourselves. No other person can improve our attitudes by somehow pouring good attitudes into our mental reservoirs.

Consider once again the significance of Viktor Frankl's conclusion that a person has the option to change his/her attitudes or state of mind. If you believe that change is possible and choose to take the necessary steps to change, marvelous results are in store for you.

A desirable attitude can be cultivated. A well-proven technique is to act-as-if. Experts believe that acting the way you wish you felt—happy, relaxed, confident, enthusiastic—can actually help you feel that way. This is a dynamic principle that produces dramatic results.[8]

For example, if you want to become an enthusiastic person, act enthusiastic even if you don't feel like it. In time you will also feel that way. What happens is that you can't act that way without thinking about it. You acquire the habit of thinking happy, relaxed, confident, and enthusiastic—getting your mind to "dwell on these things."

Enthusiastic about what? Almost anything—a hobby, a sport, a book, a service project, travel plans, friends, grandchildren, an engrossing interest of your choice. Act enthusiastic about something even if it's just hot-dogs.

Happiness is a state of mind. Dr. Frank Minirth and Dr. Paul Meier, who have coauthored a book on the subject of happiness, agree with Mark Twain who once said that people are about as happy as they make up their minds to be. Drawing on extensive research, Drs. Minirth and Meier suggest that it is desirable to learn to understand our feelings but that focusing on behavior is really the road to happiness. They make a persuasive case for generating happiness in our own lives by specific practical actions. It's clear by the title of their book *Happiness Is a Choice* that they agree with other experts who argue that we can choose our attitudes.[9]

We can grow in the direction of positive attitudes and happiness by developing new interests and activities. But too often people stop with the dream, putting off doing something about it—procrastination.

You can thwart procrastination by preparing a step-by-step plan of action. Be very specific as to just what actions are necessary to develop each new interest and activity, giving a time table for doing each one. Then take that first step and proceed. Sometimes it helps to advertise your intentions to a friend who is willing to nag you about it, if you begin to fall back into your old rut of procrastination.

There is one interest that everyone can participate in, but it's often one of the most overlooked. What is it?

An interest in and a concern for other people. It rewards one with love and friendships. There are a lot of hurting people in the world that need our love and help. But perhaps you're asking, "How does one cultivate an interest in other people?"

The answer is act it out. To make a friend, act like a friend. Delmar discovered the secret when his friend Jerry demonstrated the idea.

Delmar dropped into dark depths of self-pity when his forty-eight-year-old wife died. Unable to release his bitterness, he was contemplating suicide when Jerry, who had lost his wife years before, called him. "I didn't want to see anyone," he said, "but Jerry was so insistent that I gave up and told him to come on over."

Jerry and other people, some of them hardly more than acquaintances, wouldn't let go of Delmar. "Yeah," said Jerry, "Delmar didn't tell us about his suicidal thoughts, but we suspected. We were very concerned. At first he just sat there. Didn't want to talk. But, in time, he opened up a little, and we listened as he vented his spleen."

It took time, but eventually Jerry and the others were able to love Delmar right out of his depression. They did a lot of listening, probably the most loving and healing thing they could have done. Now Delmar has a new interest—helping others in like circumstances.

The people who don't have attitude problems in retirement are the ones who have learned to live in terms of an absorbing interest or goals that give a lasting feeling of self-fulfillment. They live for something outside themselves that they feel is important. They have found a way to satisfy their need to be needed by getting involved and thinking good thoughts before they retire— prescription and treatment that also build self-esteem.

If you cannot carry your present engrossing interests over into retirement years, you need to search now in new directions which will be satisfying and give you that lasting feeling of self-fulfillment. The younger you are when you start the easier it is.

When depressing, negative thoughts have you in their clutches and you don't have someone around like my wife to stir up your thinking, try this for starters:

Praise the Lord, O my soul, and forget not all his benefits.
He forgives all my sins and heals all my diseases;
he redeems my life from the pit and crowns me with love and
compassion.
He satisfies my desires with good things, so that my youth is
renewed like the eagle's (Ps. 103:2–5).

The rewards are enormous: strength for the bad times and
anticipation and joy for the good times; great years and exciting
living.

CHAPTER SIX

BUILDING A NEW IDENTITY

You may have battled your way to the top of the hill in your job, but as a retired "King (or Queen) of the Hill" you watch like a wounded warrior while other white knights win accolades and promotions for their achievements.

No longer in command, you have given up your power base and much of your reason for living. The challenges and the sense of accomplishment are gone, along with your earning power. Now that you are earning less money or none at all, you may gradually become aware of the mysterious psychological implications of money. For example, to a man, feeling a loss of earning capacity is almost like sexual impotence.

When you retire you surrender a part of life (the old occupation and identity and all that goes with it) in exchange for new horizons. But while you are tantalized by the siren song of retirement freedom, in the back of your mind, a feeling of loss may dull the edge of your excitement. Or your feeling may just resemble a touch of nostalgia. Regardless, even if you are accorded the honorable position of "elder statesman," it does not fully compensate for the losses.

Scrambled feelings—you want to hang on to all that was good

about the old while grabbing, with great gusto, the promise of the new.

Whether man or woman we change identities when we change occupations, retire, or make some other big change in our life. But what happens if we abandon the old comfortable identity without establishing a new one? How can we avoid the problems often associated with an identity vacuum?

Dr. Allan Fromme, a clinical psychologist and therapist with over thirty years of experience makes this observation:

> Having lived our life in a world where status and emulation, work and success, activity and effort have been conditions necessary for self-justification and social approval, how can we preserve our acceptance of self without them? . . . Worse yet, we perceive these changes as marking the final phase of our life— no more planning, reaching, building.[1]

It begins to look like the end of life. And we aren't ready for that.

SURVIVING TRANSITION TRAUMA

Relishing the first feelings of retirement is like playing hooky. Like a beautiful dream that delights the spirit, your mind flashes pictures of playing and loafing and doing what you want when you want to. These pictures are enhanced by an occasional flashback vision of those poor working slaves in Porsches and Pintos playing bumper tag as they struggle to work through rush-hour traffic.

So much for the first month.

The second month away from the job drops you back to earth like a defective parachute. Euphoria fades. And disillusionment sets in.

About this time in my own retirement, I couldn't understand the weird dichotomous thoughts that rattled around in my head.

"Could it really be true that I missed the Boss's call. What am I, a masochist? There were only two reasons the Boss ever called me: to chew my backside for a mistake or to ask me to solve a problem no one else could handle. Fortunately it was mostly the latter." Smiling, I recalled the feeling of power those calls gave me. But then the cloud of reality would throw a shadow over my consciousness.

Yesterday I wielded power and basked in the recognition that went with my position as Manager of Quality Assurance. Now it was as though I didn't exist. The things that once identified me to other people as Manager of Quality Assurance were suddenly gone—my office, my identification badge, my secretary. I didn't belong to the club anymore. I had been disconnected, drummed out of the service with only a farewell party.

I no longer tasted the pleasure of feeling like an important cog in the machinery of progress, no longer saw challenging projects completed successfully. I was, in fact, missing the tremendous gratification of meaningful accomplishment. My authority and influence were gone.

It was as if I had lost my validity as a person. I felt that a whole section of my life was gone forever—a section that gave me a recognized and valid status.

And the people I worked with, what about them? Why did I miss them? Was there anything special about them?

Yes and no. They were ordinary people, capable, conscientious, good old red-blooded American citizens who helped each other. But there was a camaraderie that developed as we worked together through experiences both good and bad. Now that is all just a memory. What can replace it? Or is replacement even necessary?

When the reverie faded, I would be back in the present. But what exactly does the "present" consist of?

Based on thirty years seniority in the position, my wife claims to be boss around the house. She has certain jobs and routines she performs in a certain way. I'm an interloper. The cat stretches, yawns, and slinks away when I make friendly overtures. My golfing partner often blows me away on the golf course. And that's not all. They're after me. My aching mind is stretched over the immutable rack of Murphy's laws. If anything can go wrong, it does, ad infinitum.

You may be among the retirees who experience such feelings. Even though the working world has lost you, a key individual, a VIP in your own right, it keeps on turning without a squeak. And your status in retirement compares unfavorably with that of a Roman galley slave. Your ego is bruised, battered, and shriveled like a prune. You feel more like a joker than a king. It's called retirement shock. You ask yourself, "Who am I anyway?"

YOU BECOME WHAT YOU DO

In our culture, work has become a compelling factor in determining personal identity. When strangers are introduced, it is often "this is John Yazboo, engineer with XYZ Corporation" or "this is Jane Tellem, professor of English at Upstate University."

Whether or not the person's work is part of the introduction, our conversation most often turns first to our occupations. We feel comfortable talking about what we do. It's nonthreatening.

We think of each other in vocational terms. It doesn't matter whether we are a plumber, engineer, airline pilot, musician, farmer, teacher, homemaker, executive, or business owner. There is a close connection between being and doing.

Yes, we may have other identities such as member or officer in our service club, a member or leader in our church or professional society. But most often we are identified with our work. We find ourselves in our work. We develop our God-given potential through our work. We gain and maintain self-respect through our work. And we derive varying degrees of satisfaction from our work and certain work-related rewards such as money, achievement, recognition, and working with people we enjoy.

Howard Shank, retired advertising executive turned author, says that we often "let our career become synonymous with life itself. It is not just a livelihood. It is sport, pastime, hobby, lover. It provides our friends and our social life. It sets our goals, defines our ambitions, gives us our report cards. Slowly, seductively, it comes to define the very word 'important.'"[2]

Thus, over the years, our work has slowly entwined itself in the very fiber of our being. The connections are strong. And looming over the retiree is the threat that these important connections will be severed. That many of the benefits we derived from our work will be forever lost.

FEELING YOUR LOSSES

The reaction to a lost identity varies greatly with the individual. Some appear to have no problem. Others experience everything from mild anxiety to frustration, health problems, depression, or all of the above.

Some people may feel that identity is only a male concern. That just isn't true—and as more women join the ranks of the employed, it's likely to become less true. Women retire, too, and go through a retirement transition. For those who have no family, a career may be the most important part of their life. Other women successfully carry on a career of homemaking and/or child raising while pursuing an outside career. Still others construct a second career after they have straightened up the kids' rooms for the last time.

So what happens to women who retire from either the outside or in-home career? Just as with men, there is no general answer. Reactions run the gamut, depending on character, personality, self-esteem, and sense of values. Some women feel a great sense of loss when they wind down their careers. Some women feel useless when their children leave home. Others are not conscious of the slightest emotional twinge in either case.

I have observed many employed women (with no less commitment to a first class job than their male counterparts) who, when they retired, let go without breaking their fingernails. Their sense of values seemed to prescribe a more graceful exit. Could it be that a woman is less likely than a man to sell her soul to the company store, so that withdrawal is less traumatic? But, just as with some men, some women sense a painful loss.

One of the most painful effects of retirement on men and women of achievement in business and the professions is the loss of position status. Top and middle management executives are likely to be people whose ego needs demand the status of a title or some other recognition, and a sense of accomplishment.

Once these achievers attain to status and power they tend to hang on at all costs. When they lose these they are likely to experience resentment and depression. Many executives miss the adrenaline flow and ego nurturing. They may suffer withdrawal symptoms, relieved only by returning to action. If they can't return to their job, which is usually the case, they seek other worlds to conquer.

Achievers are like that. Observers may think this is all vanity. But it is more than that. Their healthy egos are not so much vanity as an unshakable confidence in their own vision and capability. They usually possess a combination of optimism, energy, and enthusiasm in large measure. Not only do achievers want the personal satisfaction of continuing to use their talents, they see it as a waste if they do not.

But where do you fit into the picture?

Examine your feelings about your job before you leave it. How important is it? Does your work provide the deep and varied satisfactions which, if no longer there, would give you a feeling of deep loss? Is it the sun around which your life revolves or do you feel it is "just a job"—one you can walk away from without looking back? Any strong feelings?

You may be enjoying your work identity, but perhaps in later years you have developed a dislike for some of the boring routine which is part of nearly every job. Or while you enjoy the work and the identity, perhaps certain job pressures have become intolerable. These are just a few of the many other features of your work that may confuse your feelings.

Nearly all people will feel a loss which is directly proportional to their job satisfaction at the time of retirement. But at first, retirement euphoria may screen out such feelings. Gradually, however, the feelings of loss impinge the consciousness. If then the loss is considered significant, the transition will be painful unless certain steps are taken to avoid the trauma.

Whatever is removed from a life leaves a void and must be replaced by something else. The mental pain of our loss, whether large or small, is relieved only by filling the vacuum.

With what? And when?

SEARCHING FOR ANSWERS

For the first two years of my retirement, I honestly could not tell anyone who I was. My self-image was incoherent. When trying to explain what I was doing, I fumbled with vague, fuzzy phrases. I was bewildered. And looking back didn't help. Who I was yesterday was no more useful than the runway behind an airplane.

I was busy but moody. Questions constantly recurred in my mind. Who am I now? What kind of person am I? What kind of person do I want to be? What do I really want to do? What, in my mind, is important and worthwhile—something that will maintain my feeling of self-worth? I floundered from happy to depressed. My effort to connect with a new identity was like trying to eat soup with a fork.

My wife, God bless her, tried to help. To her my dilemma was shocking. But all her loving patience could not completely mask her occasional exasperation with my moodiness and negative attitudes. I had a plethora of options and yet felt disgruntled and frustrated. It was ludicrous. Had I lost my ability to make a decision?

Mental and emotional problems sometimes rise like a phoenix from the ashes of an abandoned career, ready to crush the joy out of the unprepared. But every situation has its own special twist. As the following stories show, some of my foresighted friends sailed serenely into a beautiful sunset. Others hunkered down for a time before they dug their way out of their dilemma.

» Walt «

Walt was ready. No early retirement was going to catch him with his head in the sand. At age sixty-two, Walt retired from his job as principal of a large high school in Oregon. But three years before he pulled the plug, he had studied for, and passed the state exam for his license as an insurance agent. Then he began his new business in his spare time.

In his position as principal and with his gregarious personality, Walt enjoyed a certain amount of community prestige. His identity nurtured his ego and satisfied his self-image. He was happy with his career but restless. Now that he qualified for a full pension, he was ready to make a change.

Walt was well known and his numerous contacts in the teaching profession were like money in the bank. His specialty was tax-sheltered annuities which the teachers gobbled up with great gusto. When he closed out his teaching career, Walt expanded his product line and sold single premium deferred annuities and life insurance. His business went from good to better to beyond his wildest dreams. His wife, Harriet worries that he may be working too hard.

Walt didn't really retire. From his former job, he "transitioned" into a flourishing business. He continued to enjoy what he called "equivalent position and prestige" in the community, slipping into his new identity as naturally as a caterpillar becomes a butterfly.

» John «

John was a high-level executive in a large corporation. During his working days, his ego was well fed. Both he and his wife enjoyed the attention accorded a man in his position.

An achiever, John felt he had done it all. But his heavy responsibilities in recent years had caused executive burn-out. He had had it up to his eyeballs with administration. Because company policy decreed that top executives retire at sixty-five, he knew exactly when he was going to leave.

Self-assured and thoughtful, John started planning early. He wanted to avoid any more stress. Since money was no problem and he had had a lifetime of recognition and prestige, he didn't seem to feel a need for any more. So he looked forward to working with his hands instead of pushing paper. He began with house and yard projects and later helped his son acquire, move into, and renovate a house. Now his time is spent on woodworking, other craftwork, and leisurely travel with his wife.

Three years later John is satisfied with his decisions. He has assumed a vastly different identity without so much as an emotional twitch—no transition trauma. However, both he and his wife concede that they had to make some adjustments to resolve conflicts brought on by their new togetherness.

» Steve «

An airline pilot, "Captain" Steve exited under protest. Mandatory retirement regulations pushed him kicking and screaming into a new identity.

Steve had received immense personal satisfaction from the title and role of airline captain. For a time before retirement, he enjoyed a manager's position with the airline. After retirement he tried some consulting jobs, but when they folded up, he became frustrated and resentful. There was nothing left but to play the role of a handyman which bent his battered ego even more. Like the person who was told to "cheer up, things could be worse," he cheered up and sure enough things got worse.

Steve had been plunged into a vacuum without an identity support system—at least without one that would not irritate his self-esteem. A situation he found impossible to accept.

Then his wife, Evelyn, heard about a businessmen's support group and talked him into joining. Through that, Steve began to systematically assess his skills and background and plan an attack on his problem. Some additional training and the contacts he had established, landed him in a consulting job with an aircraft manufacturer. When I last talked to him, he was as happy and fulfilled as the day he flew his first solo in his biplane trainer.

Steve tells me he has further plans. In his younger days, he was a journeyman carpenter, so now he is working to get his contractor's license so that he can go into the house renovation business. Steve now has big dreams and the willingness to pay the price to make them come true.

As we talked he glanced at his wife and said, "You know, it was harder on Evelyn than it was on me. It was all in my head, but she felt responsible for my happiness. The stress made her sick. She had things she wanted to do, but she spent her time trying to find a way to solve my problem. It was then I realized even more what a great person she is."

Evelyn chimed in, "It took both of us to do it. When Steve pasted his shattered ego together, I started a new career myself. I've always been interested in dress design and have dabbled in it from time to time. But now I'm doing it seriously. Things are going great, and I'm so excited I can hardly stand it."

Their only regrets are the two years they wasted wandering in the maze.

» Joanne «

Joanne, a retired teacher, describes herself as a people person. When she and her husband Andy retired to their wooded mountain home, it seemed blissful. Soon, however, she noticed the blahs creeping into her feelings. She felt she was on the verge of depression. Uncertain about the cause of these strange feelings, she thought maybe it was the change in weather. Living in the mountains meant much more rain and cloudy days, less sunshine. Too, she missed her old friends. It was much more difficult to get together with them now that they were farther away.

Joanne didn't want to worry Andy so she said nothing about her feelings. Without having the foggiest notion what she was looking for, she decided to search for something to do other than keeping house and contemplating her blissful surroundings.

Almost miraculously her feelings were transformed when she took a part-time job in a bookstore. Her smile returned, her eyes sparkled.

Andy wondered what she had been up to.

But he need not have worried. All she needed was the human contact her job provided. It enabled her to avoid what appeared to be an approaching depression.

» Bob «

Bob had to hear the second shoe drop before he realized his retirement plan was as full of holes as his work jeans. The first shoe hit the floor when his health let him down and he had to retire early. A maintenance technician for a community college, he had qualified for a pension which, along with Social Security, seemed adequate but allowed for few luxuries.

No problem, he thought. He would spend a lot of time at his daughter's home taking care of his grandsons while his daughter worked. In his spare time, he would do some golfing and some volunteer work for the church. "All of which," as his wife, Ruth put it, "keeps him entertained and out of my way."

When I asked him about possible identity problems, his response was, "What do you mean? My identity is 'grandpa' and I'm very happy with that. I really enjoy our grandsons. Besides, it makes me feel very useful. I'm doing something that is a big help to our daughter and our son-in-law."

Eight months later the other shoe dropped when his daughter and her family moved to another state. Bob and Ruth thought about following them but realized that they couldn't just keep doing that. Now Bob's identity as "grandpa" is in disarray, and he's looking for another one. He seems lost and Ruth is beginning to worry about him.

PREVENTING AN IDENTITY CRISIS

To prevent a struggle with identity crisis in your own life, you need to answer the following questions.

1. Will you miss your job: the challenges, the sense of accomplishment, the status, and the feeling of self-worth? Will you miss the people?

2. Will you miss the purposefulness, the adventure?

3. What else will you miss? The paycheck? The feeling of usefulness? The authority, the power base, the prestige?

4. How important to you are these losses? Will your self-esteem be bent out of shape by the losses? Can you be happy without them or will you need to replace some of them?

5. What kind of replacements would be satisfactory? How can you go about making the substitutions?

As a part of the exercise, rethink your values and decide what is really important. Now plan and try some things before retirement.

It is possible to learn from other people's experience but not by simply copying them. Different personalities and temperaments preclude that simple solution. Some people have no problem. Others think they won't and are quite surprised when they do. But one way to preclude an unpleasant surprise and smooth the transition into retirement is to start building a new identity before it's time for the big change.

BUILDING BLOCKS FOR YOUR NEW IDENTITY

Loafing is not the answer to your retirement identity. Neither is catching up on jobs around the old homestead. These can carry you through a couple of months or even longer, but ultimately they become tedious and b-o-r-i-n-g.

Just playing is not the answer either. Although creative, quality leisure provides one important element in zestful retirement, full-time play can be a drag.

The crisis usually occurs some months or even a year or more after the initial euphoria of retirement fades. At first there is a flurry of travel, painting the house, fixing the plumbing, reading books, mixing with other retirees (the workers are of course working), playing lots of golf or bridge, and the list goes on and on. But there's nothing with real meaning.

Not many years ago, most people who retired were in poor health or on the verge of death. Unable to do anything else, they were mostly content to just fade into the sunset. No more. The health and vigor of the late model retiree demands something else. But this also poses a problem. How can we fill those added years with exciting meaning?

People react differently to the retirement transition—the switching of identities—just as people react differently to sky diving. Some see it as a nonthreatening, exciting challenge. Others panic. Some people just suppress their feelings. Others acknowledge the feelings but accept them passively, whether good or bad.

One of the helpful developments in the current retirement scene is the opportunity many have to continue their old job part time. This allows a person the time to make adjustments, to build a bridge to a new identity before trying to cross the river. But for those who must quit or choose to quit their job cold turkey, it is not unlike trying to build a bridge while floating downstream on a raft.

Personality, experiences, value systems, ego needs, health, and all sorts of psychological factors and other circumstances play a part in how people feel about their new identity.

I was not content to accept the identity of an ex-anything. I wanted to have a current identity that did not irritate my self-esteem. One, of which I could say, "I like people to think of me as a _____." I was looking for an identity that was as satisfying as my old one—an absorbing interest that would be exciting and challenging. The mental and emotional problems I experienced came as a complete surprise. They didn't hit like stampeding elephants, but crept in quietly like invading termites.

Where did I go wrong? I didn't understand the subtle elements of identity—the involvement of self-esteem. I didn't realize the impact of the losses which come with winding down a career. And I did an inadequate job of replacing them before I retired. So after I had retired, my search for a new identity was time-consuming and painful.

But even more important, through forty years of operating in our culture, I had adopted its materialistic value system. The window through which I viewed life had been discolored and crazed so that I saw the important human values only dimly. Gathering dust in the remote corners of my mind were the treasures of human qualities like compassion, love, forgiveness, humility, sensitivity, appreciation, thankfulness, personal freedom, and inner peace.

During my transition trauma, I had to make several solo maintenance trips to our mountain cabin—three hours of driving each way, including forty miles of narrow, winding road. It provided opportunity for reflection and conversing with God. I talked and hoped God was listening to my monologue.

Fortunately, God understands plain English. My language was nothing if not plain. My anger and frustration tumbled out.

I said, "Show me some answers now. Handwriting on the wall, bells, whistles, voices, or whatever. But make it clear. All I need to know is what, where, when, and how, with options on other answers."

If he had answered the way I suggested, I'd have been scared out of my skull. But God was subtle. When my mouth ran down and stopped generating verbal fog, my mind and ears began to function, and he was able to get through quietly. An impression swept into my mind, brushing aside my mental cobwebs. Almost as clear as if I heard it with my ears, came the thought, "You're in a heap of trouble. Why not write a book about it? You can use your experience to help other people."

Writing this book has been therapeutic but it has also been a great way to tell people about the 70 percent of our preparation that we did right.

Yes, things are looking up. I'm now having the time of my life. My self-image is happy with financial consulting and writing. I'm getting in touch with some of the human values that I had been neglecting. And, more important, Alice smiles a lot.

CHAPTER SEVEN

PLANNING THE REST OF YOUR LIFE

In the military service we were sometimes warned to "shape up or ship out."

The meaning of "shape up" always came through loud and clear. But we were never quite sure what "ship out" meant. Our uncertainty conjured up all sorts of dismal and fearsome visions—a rather effective means for controlling impressionable young minds.

Shaping up for retirement is not as clearly understood as shaping up for the military. But it is just as imperative. It means preparation—not only good planning, but a training program—one that is rigorous practice for the retirement game. Let's concern ourselves first with the planning.

Your retirement plan should look ahead and focus on the exciting possibilities of your later years. This is essential, but not easy. As Chuck Swindoll so aptly expressed it, "It's easier to look back into the past and smile on yesterday's accomplishments than it is to look ahead into the future and think about tomorrow's possibilities."[1] But believe me, it is worth the effort. So don't be like one of those people who prefer to drift into retirement like a rudderless ship. They hope they are approaching some misty retirement paradise, but more than likely, they will be smashed against the rocky shore of broken dreams. They have lots of hope, but no sense of direction.

Planning your future may seem formidable because you are uncertain about how to start. A normal approach would be to visualize your expectations and write out some goals. But even before that, you should think about priorities.

> What is important to you?
> What really makes life worthwhile?

As you ponder these questions your mind will form a framework of values within which you can begin to build your plan.

RETIREMENT IS JUST ONE OPTION

Like Monday morning quarterbacks, the people who claim to know the most about retirement are often those who have never played the game. When I announced my retirement, it was incredible how much unsolicited advice I received from well-meaning friends. I was showered with diverse and conflicting opinions. If I had taken them all seriously, I would have quickly qualified for a straight jacket.

My friend John was solicitous. He confided that a study at the large XYZ Corporation concluded that the average retiree collected only eighteen monthly pension checks before cashing in his chips. Not that I take such data seriously, but seventeen months after retiring I took the precaution of having a thorough physical examination.

Evidently John took the study more seriously than I did. He is my age and still working. Several other people my age that I worked with at the time of my retirement decided they had no good reason to retire. They enjoyed their work more than anything else they could think of and opted to continue. So if you feel that way, why retire?

Why indeed! People were not designed for retirement, if by the term *retirement* we mean "stop." But in the past few years, the term *retirement* has taken on new meaning. As used now by the new breed of mature persons, it more often means "change" rather than "stop." It means trading in your present occupation for a new challenge. And because of the many exciting opportunities for personal fulfillment, most people choose this change even when they also have the option not to.

Many psychologists recommend that we periodically evaluate our lives. Where we are, where we have been, where we are going, and who we are. Even without any big changes on the horizon, this is a good idea. But it's especially true when a crisis looms or a major change, either voluntary or involuntary, upsets our life. And it doesn't matter whether it involves a physical or mental displacement from where we have been, or whether it's expected or unexpected. At such times it becomes very important, and often urgent, to thoroughly review our present state in the process of planning our future course.

Retirement is definitely such a time.

For any change as momentous as retirement you should have good reasons. So if you plan to retire just because it seems to be the expected thing to do, recheck your thinking and disregard the "standard" reasons for retiring. Your reasons for retiring should be your own, not somebody else's.

Many people think of retirement in terms of what they are retiring *from*. That's not important. The secret to successful retirement is to think in terms of what you would like to retire *to*.

Life is not what you did yesterday. What was best for earning money isn't necessarily best for your enjoyment. Try thinking in new ways: do some brainstorming. Your thoughts don't have to follow the same old gray matter grooves. Neither do you have to act in the same old predictable way. Loosen up. Enjoy the freedom.

I realize that doing what you want to do takes some getting used to. But if you will venture out and do something you always wanted to do but never had the time, resources or visceral fortitude to do, you will rediscover your individuality.

ANSWERING THE RELEVANT QUESTIONS

There's no better way to rev up the brain cells than to contemplate the questions you will need to answer as you begin to design your retirement scenario! The following list is only a sample of things to consider. To provide at least a modicum of fairness, invite your spouse to help you find the answers.

▶ What income will we need?
▶ What income will we have?
▶ How will we reconcile the difference?
▶ Where will we live?
▶ Can my spouse and I cope with seeing much more of each other?
▶ What will I do when I retire?

Sit in a rocking chair on the front porch.

Watch TV.

Knit or whittle.

Travel.

Spend more time fishing and/or playing tennis, golf, bridge.

Visit the children.

Babysit the grandchildren.

Take care of aging parents.

Work part time.

Start a business.

All or a smattering of the above.

▶ Am I temperamentally suited to the retirement I envision?

▶ Will what I do satisfy my psychological needs relative to ego, identity, and the need to be needed? Will it be worthwhile?

▶ Will my spouse be happy with what I/we choose to do?

By now it's probably apparent to you that answering these questions is what planning is all about. Obviously, depending on your circumstances, you may have many other questions that need answers. Using this list as a starting point, customize one to fit your own situation. Remember it's important to write out your questions and keep them where they can be quickly retrieved for future reference. Keep them with other planning papers. Then as you go about your planning, refer to them occasionally to make sure you are making progress toward their answers.

HOW TO FRAME YOUR RETIREMENT PLAN

Writing a plan may be your least favorite occupation. But it's surprising how exciting it can be when you get into the spirit of it. For one thing, you can dream with a purpose. It's like planning a wonderful trip to that place you have always wanted to visit, except it's more important.

Your retirement plan should be as personal as your fingerprints. It consists primarily of answers to your questions and a how-to scheme for reaching your goals. It's a program for assuring that your later years will truly be vintage years. So before you start writing the plan it is best to make a list of those questions we talked about in the previous section.

Don't be intimidated by the fact that you can't possibly think of all contingencies at this time. Your plan is intended to be a living document. As you progress through your middle years, your plan should be updated to adapt to any new ideas.

And don't just carry your ideas around in your head. Record them on paper. There is nothing quite like a written plan to focus your energy. Like examining a diamond through a microscope, a plan will also reveal flaws in your thinking.

Furthermore, writing out your ideas makes a deeper impression on your conscious mind which in turn programs your powerful subconscious mind. Your subconscious then goes to work implementing your plan. Of course, you will have to work, too.[2]

In broad terms, your plan should consist of three parts:

1. *Objectives and goals.* Your dreams, large and small. Long-term objectives and short-term goals.

2. *Answers to your questions.* Tentative, as seen from where you are now.

3. *A program of action.* What you need to do to reach your goals. Specific actions with a time schedule.

That's the big picture. From a practical standpoint, writing a plan is more manageable if you write it in sections. At least for a first cut. For example, one section might deal with financial plans; another with career change or employment plans; another with continuing education; and another with relationships—how you will cope with aging parents, children, etc.

Each section should have the three parts as listed above. Since the sections are synergistic, their interrelationships must eventually be considered and all combined into your overall plan.

Your first plan will not be, nor does it need to be, a work of art. All you are looking for is something practical. Whatever it is, it should be periodically updated. My suggestion is to update every three years before the age of fifty, every two years from ages fifty to fifty-five, and every year thereafter.

I urge you to start now. It is unlikely that anyone else will do your planning for you—not the government, not a guardian angel, not your parents, not your children, not anyone but you.

EXPECTANT DREAMING—AN EXERCISE

For those who do not know exactly what they want to do with the rest of their life, it's now dream time. No doubt, you've been doing some of that already. Almost everyone has tucked away some dreams in the back of their minds that they can dust off now and think seriously about pursuing. But I am talking about serious dreaming, not just will-o'-the-wisps.

One of the dynamic ways to start your motor is to use what Dr. Joyce Brothers calls the "Quick List Technique."[3]

Get a sheet of paper and pencil. Then, quickly, write down the three things you want most in the world at this particular moment. Don't stop to think. Write as fast as the ideas pop into your mind.

You're not through yet. Dr. Brothers suggests that you put your list away in some place from which you can easily retrieve it. One week later again write a quick list—your three wishes at that particular time. Save this new list. Repeat this process for the next six to eight weeks. At the end of that time, gather all the lists together and study them.[4]

You will see a pattern. As you study the lists, you will have a clearer idea of what you want most in the world. These, of course, are tentative and will likely be modified over time. Our wants usually change with age and stage. People who experience personal growth are bound to change their ideas of what is important. Hence, a change in goals.

Dr. Brothers adds this perspective: "Men and women with potential have many goals, and these goals shift from time to time. Don't feel that you are locked into working for something just because you decided a year ago that that was what you wanted. If you want to change course, go ahead. Change. Just be sure that you are the one in charge of your life."[5]

As you go through this expectant dreaming exercise, fix in your mind the two questions raised in the first part of this chapter. They will frame your dream:

What really makes life worthwhile?
What is really important to you?

Don't slough off that word *important*. Importance is in the mind of the thinker. Is there something on which you are willing to spend your precious retirement years? Work of some kind? Relationships? A long-held dream? What gives you a thrill, a sense of great accomplishment, or the satisfaction of helping a fellow human?

Now rev up your thinking machine with three more questions:

What gives you your feeling of self-esteem?
What fulfills your need to be needed?
What are your high priority values?

Retirement adjustment includes attitudes, value system, and priorities. If you think in depth about these before retirement, your adjustment may take place without a glitch.

HOW TO SELECT YOUR GOALS

Now you are ready to use the chart in figure 7.1 to organize your dreams and wishes into goals. This chart is intended to be a five-year working document—one you can revise periodically.

At this stage of planning, we are talking about long-term, big-picture goals—the big dreams. Why not dream big? Big dreams cost no more than little ones. There's time enough later to get practical when you plan the implementation of these dreams with specific objectives and actions.

The right-hand column of the chart in figure 7.1 shows two things: (1) the importance to you of each particular goal relative to the other goals (5 being the most important and *1* being the least important), and (2) the five years from 1988 to 1992. To use the chart, put a number from 1 to 5 in the column under the appropriate year opposite each of the big dream goals you have

Big Dream Goals	Importance to You 1 to 5				
	1988	1989	1990	1991	1992

Figure 7.1. Organizing dreams into goals.

written in. Now you can use this chart to record your goals over the next five years and see how they change, if they do.

To stimulate your thinking, here are some possible long-term, big-dream goals. These may not be the type of things that interest you at all, but they will give you an idea what I am talking about.

▶ Continue full-time work (paid or unpaid).

▶ Work part time (paid or unpaid).

▶ Help others through volunteer work.

▶ Achieve status and/or fame.

▶ Learn and grow in new directions.

▶ Be open to opportunities.

▶ Cultivate friendships.

▶ Spend more time with family.

▶ Achieve financial independence.

▶ Play and travel.

The purpose of the chart is for you to make your own selections based on the results of your quick list exercise and other brainstorming methods.

You will probably have several goals, but they may vary in importance. This exercise should help you set priorities in your pursuit of goals. The chart has enough room so that you can add some new goals if and when you change your mind. Keep in mind, however, that some of these goals may conflict. For example, if you give a high value to full-time paid work, it may be unrealistic for you to give a high priority to spending a lot of time helping others.

The next step in this goal-selecting process is to take those goals which you feel are most important and write them out in detail. To keep track of changes in your desires, you should repeat this process occasionally, perhaps once a year. When you spot changes, seriously analyze the possible reasons. Have your goals really changed? Do the changes reflect growth or a loss of vision and determination?

In chapter 8, we will see how to work toward these goals by setting specific, short-term objectives, and we'll also take a look at how some other people have worked toward meaningful later years.

Attainment of any worthwhile goal exacts a price. The cost may be in terms of time, money, compromises, or giving up something else less important to you. If you're serious about the goal, be willing to pay the price.

CHAPTER EIGHT

STRATEGY FOR GROWING IN NEW DIRECTIONS

Mavis was excited. Her eyes sparkled as she told me she had decided to go back to college. But then her expression changed to one of concern, and she said, "I'm a little worried that I might not be able to compete with the younger generation. I don't know if I can hack it."

At the time she talked to me, several years ago, Mavis was a middle-aged married woman who had managed the household and raised the children while her husband was pursuing his career.

When she and her husband were first married, she had dropped out of college. Now the children were grown and she had time to complete her interrupted education. Dreaming of a late life career and knowing of my experience of going to college in later life (I got my M.S. degree at age fifty), she decided to sample my reaction to her dream.

Despite her strong desire and excitement at the prospect, Mavis expressed a fear that many older people have. In her mind, doubt and fear competed for supremacy with hope and determination. She wondered whether the dream could ever become a reality.

Can I pick up where I left off?
Have I lost the capability that I once had?
Can I compete with the young tigers of this technological age?
Is it really worth the effort?

After hearing her questions, I climbed on my soapbox and expounded. "Mavis, we mature people have just as many 'smarts' as the younger people have. Furthermore, due to our experience, we often have a greater desire and a more focused drive. We are usually more certain of what we want. We can reach our goals with less wheel-spinning.

"As to whether it is worth the effort, consider the alternative, namely, your regrets for not taking the chance when you see other people doing it and loving it—when you see them come alive while you curl up in the fetal position and abort. It is indeed worth the effort. Go for it!"

She did. She found it exciting to get graded for something she did for herself. And it wasn't folding socks or washing dishes. Three years later she was the proud possessor of a B.A. degree in psychology. She was on her way.

DEVELOPING A NEW CAREER

Despite her original fear, Mavis was willing to face possible failure. She had the visceral fortitude to try, and subsequently realized her great dream—a B.A. degree. But that was just the beginning.

Mavis' first career was a combination of managing a home and nurturing a family. With this experience and her training in psychology, she has now accepted a position as Intern Re-entry

Advisor and Counselor for Older Students at a state university while working toward an M.A. degree in counseling and education. Mavis is off and running in a new career.

» Jeff and Betty «

Jeff at one time was Chief Operations Officer for a small manufacturing plant. For several years after retiring from that career, he consulted for various corporate executives on management problems. Jeff's wife Betty had never been employed outside of their home. She was the homemaker and child raiser. But now the children were grown, and when Jeff switched careers once again, Betty joined him. They were both sixty-five years old when they studied for, and passed, the real-estate license exam. Sixty-eight years young, they are now a team of successful realtors.

» Norm and Margaret «

Norm, who enjoyed a successful engineering career was born a few years too soon. When he turned sixty-five, he was caught in the clutches of archaic retirement laws. Mandatory retirement at sixty-five was still legal. Things never looked more bleak to Norm than when he was shoved kicking and screaming into a retirement for which he was totally unprepared. Due to his lack of financial planning, Norm was completely dependent on an inadequate pension.

By his own admission a procrastinator, Norm had had vague misgivings about not having anything to do in retirement. But he hadn't done anything about it. He had not cultivated any outside interests. Here he was in the eighth inning of his life with two strikes against him, and he was "caught looking" as life's fast ball smoked across the plate. Called out, Norm walked dejectedly into the retirement dugout. But there was one more inning.

A few months of retirement and both Norm and his wife Margaret were leaving footprints on walls and ceiling. Then he stumbled onto a consulting job. For the last few years, he has been happy with his new career. Now at the age of seventy-seven, Norm is tired. But he declares that he can't afford to retire. Fumbled finances fractured his dream of late-life leisure. But that's not the only problem. He still hasn't cultivated any other interests. What would he do? Vegetate? He's afraid to retire.

Norm intends to die with his boots on. That is not necessarily bad. The unpleasant part is that he has no other choice. He has lost control of his life.

You may have concluded that my definition of a new career carries with it the requirement of pay. That's not my intention. Of course, there is a lot of satisfaction in getting paid for your effort, and if you need the money, pay makes a second career that much more attractive. But for purposes of this discussion, whether or not you get paid for your work is not the key to a new career.

A hobby may start out as just that. A pleasurable diversion and change of pace from one's primary vocation. Upon your retirement, it may become a second career.

The line of demarcation between a hobby and a second career is fuzzy and difficult to define. I think the determining factor is your intention—the way you look at it. A hobby becomes a new career in the mind of the doing person. If you engage in a systematic effort to make progress and to succeed, if you strive for excellence in the performance and enjoyment of your hobby, and if it is an absorbing interest that has meaning for you, then it qualifies in my mind as a new career.

Darrell has found himself so engrossed in his volunteer work that he considers it a new career. Enabled by fortunate financial circumstances to retire comfortably at age fifty-five, he not only does one-on-one counseling with teen-agers, but he is a member of the board of several community service organizations. He is in demand by churches and other organizations as a speaker, inspiring help for the "throw away" children of our society. For this he receives no money. His pay is in the form of the immense personal satisfaction that comes from being able to make a difference. He helps a lot of hurting people, especially teen-agers and children, to gain new hope and grow into happy productive citizens.

FACING UP TO THE THREAT OF CHANGE

As with any big change in your life, a late-life career change or some form of retirement can fill you with apprehension. What if things don't work out as you hope? Your feelings may swirl in an absurd mixture of anxiety and exhilaration as you approach closer and closer to the decisive moment. But don't be alarmed. These feelings merely prove how normal you are. As Gail Sheehy expressed it in her book *Passages:*

> It would be surprising if we didn't experience some pain as we leave the familiarity of one adult stage for the uncertainty of the next. But the willingness to move through each passage is equivalent to the willingness to live abundantly. If we don't change, we don't grow. If we don't grow, we are not really living. Growth demands a temporary surrender of security. It may mean a giving up of familiar but limiting patterns, safe but unrewarding work, values no longer believed in, relationships that have lost their meaning. As Dostoevsky put it, "taking a new step, uttering a new word, is what people fear most." The real fear should be of the opposite course.[1]

Drawing heavily on his professional experience as a practicing psychiatrist, Dr. M. Scott Peck feels that, despite the occasional painful experience, change gives life spirit and significance. It injects an essence into our lives that enables us to reach a higher level of self-understanding and loving relationships.[2]

Rattle your cage. Break out. Escape from a dull routine. Grow in new directions. Allow the challenge and excitement of change to permeate your being with new scenes, new experiences, new feelings.

JOLTED OUT OF A RUT

If change is the essence of life, exactly how can we capture and exploit this energizing element?

It is easier said than done. The ruts we have dug through incessant routine are deep. Often lined with all sorts of creature comforts, they mesmerize us into a state of apathy bordering on lifelessness.

It has been said that a rut is a grave with the ends knocked out. The story is told of a man who having worked late was walking home through the pitch-black night. He chose to take a shortcut through the cemetery. Not being able to see the path, he wandered off and fell into a freshly dug grave. It was deep, and his efforts to climb out were unsuccessful. Finally exhausted, he sat down in a corner to wait for daylight and help.

Sometime later another man, having chosen to walk through the cemetery, fell into the same open grave. This second man immediately tried with all his might to scramble out, not knowing in the blackness that the first man was there. Suddenly a voice behind him said, "You'll never make it." But he did.

A timely jolt can propel you out of a rut. My wish for you is that you will be jolted from time to time by life, and that you will be faced with the need to make new departures—to move in new directions. In that way, when you reach the age of retirement, change will no longer be fearsome. Instead, you will be able to welcome it with excitement as you would an old friend.

But even when the change is not feared, deciding just what to do in your later years can be a formidable hurdle. You may have difficulty with the decision and transition simply because of the multiplicity of options—a real smorgasbord. You may want to taste everything on the table before you select an entree. There's nothing wrong with pampering your palate. But be sure to follow up in good time with a complete meal that will really nourish your retirement.

While you are gorging on a smorgasbord, others like Norm may be starving because they have not developed a taste for anything outside of their work. A certain amount of floundering is perfectly normal. But I believe that it is important to select something and try it. You can always change your mind and switch directions.

Now before you plunge in and splash around in some other person's swimming pool, be sure to review your goals. The ones you worked out in chapter 7. They may point you toward an entirely different sport—toward some special mountain you want to climb or some humanitarian service you want to perform. Base your decisions on your own goals, recognizing that they can be changed if you begin to grow in a different direction.

WINDING DOWN

For some people retirement will not lead to a new career, but rather a winding down of the old one followed, perhaps, by travel, hobbies, and sports.

One man viewing retirement from the working side said, "When I retire I'm going to do absolutely nothing, and that only part time." The people that feel that way may be burned out or just tired. And if they are frustrated or bored with their job, they can easily conclude that full-time leisure would be their pie in the sky.

For me, engaging in a wild, marvelous flurry of inactivity has only short-time appeal. Seldom are retirees happy with a life of nothing but leisure. For a time, doing nothing but play can be a refreshing step in the winding-down process. But for most people, such a life eventually becomes a hollow shell, boring and meaningless. And a feeling of worthlessness gradually crowds out the original freedom euphoria.

That having been said, let me hasten to add that retirement

ideally is a dynamic transition stage in our lives. It can be an ever-changing panorama of exciting experiences. I encourage you to flow with your feelings. If you get tired, bored, or disillusioned with what you are doing, try something else. Change course. You may even want to change your goals.

Many companies are now easing the transition into retirement by offering part-time employment or consulting contracts. I know a number of people who have elected to wind down in this way. Before retiring, even if you think you are not interested in this idea, be sure to investigate all possible options with your employer. You may be pleasantly surprised at the opportunities.

It is a great privilege to be in a position to slow down gradually instead of having to give up one's work abruptly. But it may have a couple of unfavorable features. In the first place, there is the question of motivation. Are you expressing a refusal to grow old or a refusal to give up a flattering role? Do you have a need to cling to the past instead of growing toward the future?

A second possible negative effect to consider is that continuing part-time work in your old job divides your attention and scatters your energy. Then only part of you can carry out those tantalizing retirement ideas you have floating around in your head. When Kenneth tried to do both, he felt like he was stretched over a barrel of frustration. He didn't have enough time or energy to do satisfactorily all the things he wanted to do. Six months later he quit his old job for good.

So winding down in the old job isn't for everyone. But it can be particularly attractive for people whose new retirement ideas haven't yet jelled—the people who really need more time to try some ideas before cutting loose from the old job and devoting themselves 100 percent to new activities.

There are many other possible transitions. I know several engineers that have enjoyed great personal satisfaction in alleviating a teacher shortage. They have taught everything from high school math to college engineering courses, part time, both before and after retiring. Sam, also a private pilot, now teaches a physics course. He told me that part-time teaching was the best prescription for a perfect landing he could have imagined.

Ellen accepted a part-time consulting job with the school district from which she had retired. Always interested in (and with considerable talent for) teaching music, she took over a job that many elementary teachers feel incapable of doing. For a five year wind-down, she taught music to elementary school children. Besides filling her need to be needed and providing some additional income, it was a great way to maintain contact with teacher friends.

Janet, Beth, and Warren are three other teachers who have worked for their school districts part time after they retired and started receiving their pensions. Janet conducted a special kindergarten level test program. Beth prepared a curriculum for a new spelling program. Warren is teaching high school algebra and geometry for the equivalent of half time. This kind of opportunity is becoming common practice in certain school districts in California.

But I extend a word of caution here so that you won't be unpleasantly surprised. There may be limits (as there are in the Social Security system) as to what you can earn without losing some of your pension benefits. Whatever the source of your retirement benefits, be sure to check this out.

The opportunities for winding down are limitless. It's an exciting time to retire. But it does take some initiative on your part. You need to look for opportunities, talk to people, and keep your eyes and ears open.

A final thought for this subject. I think an extended vacation at the time of retirement is a good idea. Choose something that appeals to you: travel, fishing, golf, or whatever. Savor your new freedom. It uncouples you from a runaway locomotive and shunts you onto a siding where your mind can relax in a state of receptiveness and anticipation, excited but not driven. In fact, some retirees choose to keep right on traveling for years rather than searching for new worlds to conquer. For others it's just a time to recharge their batteries and clear their vision.

DISCOVERING HIDDEN TALENTS AND INTERESTS

This struggle we call "making a living" has a way of burying some of our talents and interests. Oh yes, we may have stretched and grown in many ways through our career. But few people use all their talents and interests in their vocation. Hopefully, the unused talents are not rusted beyond salvaging.

How well do you know yourself? What are the things that give you the greatest deep-down satisfaction and joy?

Let's sift through the sands of time and then do some brainstorming. Here are some questions to get you started:

How did you spend your spare time as a teen-ager?
What sports or hobbies did you enjoy most?
What extracurricular activities did you participate in while you were in school?
What were the subjects that turned you on?
Did you receive special recognition for either academic work or extracurricular activities?
What other interests did you have in your early life? Did you receive recognition for any of them?
What were your outstanding personal qualities in your youth?
Did you enjoy trying new things?

Now update the scenario to the present:

What talents or hobbies have you developed?
What skills and interests have you developed as part of your vocation?
What are your strengths and weaknesses?
What have you always wanted to do but for lack of time, money, or guts have not done?

Brainstorm these by yourself, with your spouse, and/or with a noncritical friend. Keep records. Over time, some ideas will emerge from which you can prepare a list. This list is different from, but supports, the list of long-term (big-dream) goals you prepared in chapter 7. List activities, interests, and enterprises which, if you pursue (one or more), will advance you toward your goals and objectives. For example, if one of your goals is to work part time, this list should have one or more specific work ideas such as real estate agent, teacher of computer science, furniture maker, or continuing part time in your present occupation. This is a brainstorming list. It should include all your interests whether or not you presently have the skill and training for their performance.

Now mark off three columns on a piece of paper as shown in figure 8.1. Then select from the list that you just prepared those options in which you feel the deepest interest and record them in the left column. You can choose as many as your judgment dictates.

With a little research, you can fill in the middle column. You may already have the training and experience to engage in some of these activities. Others may require extensive preparation. In the third column, indicate whether or not you are already qualified.

I have filled in the middle column in figure 8.1 with some examples just to give you the idea. Since requirements vary in different states and every person's situation is different, these are not intended to indicate precisely what training and experience you would need. You must determine that for yourself.

When you realize the time and effort necessary to pursue some of these activities, you may feel like deleting some of them immediately. But don't be too hasty. Give each sufficient thought so that you are making a careful, rational decision. Remember that you don't have to become a top expert in these things in order to enjoy them. Let the ideas simmer awhile.

Options	Training & Experience	Qualified (yes or no)
Financial Planner	CFP certificate, Registered investment advisor & experience	
Family Counselor	B.A./M.A. degrees in psychology, License & Internship	
Build Furniture	Woodworking interest, skills & tools	
Real Estate Agent	License, sponsor, experience	
Teaching	B.A./M.A. or other degrees, teaching certificate, experience	
Any Hobbies		
Volunteer for ___		
You Name It ___		

Figure 8.1.   Worksheet on options and qualifications.

Then weigh the pros and cons of the price you must pay in terms of time, effort, and sacrifice to prepare for each option.

What are your feelings about these?

What is your motivation for your interest in the first place?

Did you put the option on the list just because someone else suggested it or is doing it successfully?

Is your interest genuine and deep or just a passing fancy?

Now review your options and their cost in time, money, and effort. Any of the options for which you are unwilling to pay the price should be crossed off your list.

But what about your goals—the ones you worked so hard to define in chapter 7? Any of the options which are not in line with your goals should be crossed off your list or else your goals need to be reconsidered and perhaps changed. Sometimes this exercise reveals unexpressed goals you didn't know you had.

Narrow your selections down to three or four preferred options. Now put the lists away and let your subconscious go to work. But also talk to people about your ideas. They may bring up something you hadn't thought of.

SHAPING YOUR ACTION
AND STARTING YOUR MOTOR

After letting things simmer for a while, you can make a final selection of two or three options (perhaps more depending on what they are) and prepare to pursue them.

Now comes one very important step. Make an action item list along with a schedule. (See figure 8.2.) The actions listed will be

Option	Action	Start Date	Finish Date
A			
B			
C			

Figure 8.2.   Worksheet for action item list with schedule.

those you must take to put a "yes" in the qualification column opposite your final option selections in the worksheet you did on options and qualifications (figure 8.1). Let's say, for example that you have selected three and have labeled them A, B, and C. Next you will need to fill in the information called for on the worksheet in figure 8.2. Then decide on the sequence in which you will take the actions and the dates when you plan to start and complete each one. Then go for it.

CHAPTER NINE

SMOOTHING THE ROAD WITH ROBUST HEALTH

My ears are ringing. I don't remember when it started. It doesn't sound like a telephone or burglar alarm. It seems to come from inside my head. And what am I doing down here under these bushes? Strange. I feel pain but I'm not sure where it's coming from. As I look up from my position under the juniper bushes, I see the blue sky, the rain gutter on our house, and what looks like a ladder lying at a crazy angle across the bushes and planter-box. How did it get there, and why? These mysteries trouble my befuddled brain. I must find answers.

Slowly I crawl out from under the junipers, hurting in more places than a centipede with fallen arches. The world appears a bit fuzzy. I stand up. No broken legs. As I brush juniper needles out of my hair and off of my clothes, I feel pain and numbness in several extremities, but nothing seems to be broken.

Now it is coming back. I remember squatting on the edge of the roof and reaching down to paint the rain gutter. That finished, I stepped from the roof to the ladder. But it slipped away from my foot. My clutching fingers found nothing but air, space, and assorted obstacles between me and the ground.

So much for impromptu skydiving. This little episode was the culmination of our house-painting project which we started shortly after I retired. Both the ladder and I suffered an ignominious upset because of my carelessness in bracing the ladder. However, much as I hate to admit it, deterioration of my physical agility made me an accident waiting to happen.

As it turned out my ego suffered more damage than my body. On the way down I struck a planter box that is attached to the house, but it was a glancing, scraping blow. Afterward, one side of my rib cage and arm turned a deep purple and a cracked rib was very painful for about a week, not to mention several other colorful bruises and a twisted knee. The force of my fall was partially broken by shrubs, and I hit the ground flat on my back.

Some people I know have not been so fortunate. Retirees often attempt numerous projects around the home which they have previously neglected or have hired done by others. At this particular time in life, one's physical ability may have deteriorated with age and neglect precisely at the same time that there is greater opportunity for potential accidents.

This body-bruising experience got my attention. I began thinking about health just a fraction of a second after my head began to recover from its ground-thumping fall. But, of course, good health in later years is much more than avoiding accidents.

WHOLENESS AND WELLNESS—MIND, BODY, AND SPIRIT

Ever since Adam and Eve were booted out of the Garden of Eden, people have been asking, "What makes us sick and what will keep us well?" These are still challenging questions. In all the thousands of intervening years, no one has ever come up with a complete answer.

Theories abound. Some say you are what you eat. Others say you are what you think. Others claim that healthy habits are the answer—no smoking, drinking, or drugs. There are the exercise nuts, of which I am one, that espouse the benefits of exercise at any age. And then there are the gene worshipers who tell us that long-lived ancestors are the prerequisite to a long, healthy life.

Who's right? The state of our present knowledge indicates that, to some extent, they are all right. No one criterion will determine the state of your health any more than the length of a dog's tail will tell you how fast he can run.

Which is more important, the quality of life or the quantity? Would you rather die happy at age sixty-five or endure the misery of "organ recitals" and pity parties till eighty-five? Your answer is probably the same as mine. I want the best of both worlds— health and happiness until death at a very advanced age.

One bit of cheery news for those planning their later years is that the primary cause of illness is not old age. More and more doctors and scientists are convinced that, from youth to old age, physical well-being is more a matter of the state of mind and spirit than it is of chronological years.

Isn't it amazing that we keep rediscovering wisdom that has been known for centuries. Over two thousand years ago, the writer of Proverbs declared, "A cheerful heart is a good medicine, but a crushed spirit dries up the bones" (Prov. 17:22).

» Justin «

Justin, in his mid fifties, was fed up with his job and decided to change careers. He thought it would be as easy as it had been at age forty. After three months, disillusioned, and with no offers equivalent to his old position, he concluded in his own mind that no one wanted him and that he was at the end of the trail. He began to feel tired and lethargic and worried about his health; the dry bones were rattling. With the help of a doctor and an understanding wife, he persevered and after several months he unearthed some business opportunities that appealed to him. His symptoms soon disappeared and today he is his old confident self.

Studies by doctors and scientists are proving a connection between illness and such things as loneliness, hopelessness, fear, resentment, emotions, and stress. Wellness, on the other hand, is aided and abetted by such things as joy, positive attitudes, faith, hope, a good self-image, and an engrossing purpose—a reason for living.

For many years, Dr. O. Carl Simonton and his psychologist wife, Stephanie Matthews Simonton, have been treating cancer patients. Their studies produced strong indications that certain combinations of traits make some people especially vulnerable to cancer. "Hidden 'negative emotions,' the theory says, are ultimately expressed at the level of the cell." For more about their work, I refer you to the September 1980 issue of *Psychology Today* for the article by Maggie Scarf titled "Images That Heal."[1]

Bruce Larson in his book *There's a Lot More to Health Than Not Being Sick* explores this subject in considerable detail. Among his examples of research projects is the following:

> One of the oldest research projects exploring the relationship between mind, spirit, and body has been going on for the past thirty-eight years among a group of men who were college sophomores in an Eastern university in the 1940s. Investigators have been making periodic checks on the physical and mental health of this group. Their findings indicate that poor mental health is a key predicter of early physical deterioration, according to Dr. George Valliant of the psychiatry department at Cambridge Hospital in Cambridge, Massachusetts. Of forty-eight men who had the worst mental health between the ages of twenty-one and forty-six, eighteen were hit with chronic illness or death by the age of fifty-three.[2]

But you may protest, "Which came first, the poor mental health or the physical illness?"

Dr. Valliant speaks to that question. He says that it was not a matter of bad health affecting the mental state such as happiness and adjustment. Rather, the research records show that the men with the worst health in their fifties were poorly adjusted before their physical health started to deteriorate.

Another startling conclusion reached by the study was that, contrary to what we often assume, alcohol and tobacco use, obesity, and the life-span of parents and grandparents are not the most important determining factors in health and longevity. He adds that while these factors undoubtedly had some effect on the men's physical well-being, their mental health seemed to predetermine their physical health independently, or at least predominate over the other determinants.[3]

However, Dr. Valliant and other investigators agree that no matter how powerfully our mental and emotional condition influence the state of our physical health, bad habits, poor nutrition, and genes contribute to the problems. In fact, they will accelerate our demise. It is, therefore, worth the effort to take a reasonable and sound approach to good health.

MAINTAINING PHYSICAL FITNESS

Certainly it's not all in the mind. There are many diseases and circumstances that cause physical illness or injury which must be treated by a physician using drugs, surgery, or other tools of the medical profession. We are fortunate in this country to have available health care second to none.

But there are also many things we can do for ourselves in the way of illness prevention which can reduce our dependence on professional medical help. The pay-offs are increased vitality and quality living, as well as a reduction in medical expenses.

Studies sponsored by the American Heart Association and others have now proven beyond doubt that hypertension and high cholesterol are killers. And the longer you delay doing anything about these problems, the more likely you are to suffer premature heart attacks and strokes. The younger you are when you do things right, the better chance you have for delightfully healthy middle and later years.

So then the question is this: Once we have our heads screwed on right, what other factors are there in healthy aging?

The American Medical Association Family Medical Guide has suggested three broad rules for physical fitness:[4]

1. Avoidance of harmful intake, such as smoking and the immoderate use of alcohol and other harmful substances;
2. Regular exercise;
3. Proper nutrition, i.e., balanced diet and weight control.

Whatever can be said about item one applies at any age. Most adults are well aware of the harmful things that should be avoided. My advice is simple. Don't. Prevention is much easier than cure. But at the same time, I recognize that anyone already addicted to harmful substances has a very real and difficult problem. And there's no easy answer but to admit the problem and seek the help of professionals and support organizations— all much easier said than done.

Now let's explore rules two and three in more detail, beginning with rule three.

NUTRITION—EATING TO LIVE

Most of us mature adults know the difference between good and bad food. We have been exposed to good nutrition knowledge. But we are also continually enticed by high-pressure ads pushing foods that make us drool, but would be better left uneaten.

It seems that until recently the medical profession assigned a very low priority to the nutritional approach to physical and emotional health. More medical doctors are now receiving training in nutrition and recognize its tremendous contribution to good health. If your doctor isn't one of them, I suggest you find one who is.

Many doctors and nutritionists believe that good nutrition may be able to delay, or help you to avoid entirely, some disorders commonly caused by nutritional deficiencies. The biggest problem is having enough determination to eat the good and avoid the bad. Poor foods often attract the taste buds like a game of chance attracts a gambler.

For most people a well-planned diet need not be exotic or anything beyond balanced nutrition. However, for those people who have some special problem, such as obesity or diabetes, a diet should be especially tailored to their needs.

I deplore fad type diets—those which are touted as the answer to everyone's needs. I think such diets have done a lot of harm, sidetracking people from the main road to good nutrition. A lot of gullible people are experimenting with diets which are actually hazardous to their health.

For those who have a special health problem, I strongly recommend that before dieting, your first stop should be at your doctor's office, not at the bookstore or magazine stand. And when a friend tells you about a wonderful new diet that is guaranteed to cure all problems from falling hair to athlete's foot and make you look ten years younger, listen politely and then ignore it.

For those who have no special problem but are just interested in eating good nutritious food, I recommend two actions:

▶ Discuss diets with your doctor or a nutritionist on the staff of a clinic or hospital and
▶ Educate yourself.

There are many sources of good menus. One is Weight Watchers. Another is Dr. Werner Graendorf's book *A Happy Look at Aging.* His book is packed with suggestions and charts that provide a good basis for planning your own meals. Also included is a smorgasbord of good, references which will whet your appetite for further knowledge.[5]

Another good way to start your education is to read Dr. Stuart Berger's new book, *How To Be Your Own Nutritionist.*

Dr. Berger thoroughly analyzes the question of vitamins. He concludes that there are both benefits and risks in taking supplemental vitamins.

He addresses the fact that, since much nutritional value is lost in modern processing and cooking, balanced diets are not what they used to be. Furthermore, our vitamin needs are partly tied to the aging changes in our bodies. As we age, our physiological systems change and this influences the efficiency with which our bodies use vitamins. Thus our risk of vitamin deficiency increases with age.[6]

Evidence is piling up that vitamins may play a larger role in inhibiting disease than it was previously thought. "At Harvard, researchers studied more than 1200 elderly men and women and found that those who eat a lot of vegetables containing beta-carotene (a form of vitamin A) are far less likely to get cancer than those who don't." [7] The study also showed that depression seems to be more likely when B-6 levels are lower than average.

Dr. Berger cites many other studies to support the use of supplemental vitamins. But he also reveals a negative side of the question. More and more people seem to think that if a little is good, much is better. Some are taking vitamins and minerals many times over the safe limits, and reports of toxicity are increasing. Side effects of overdosing can include liver damage and neurologic damage among other undesirable effects. The specific effect depends on the amount and the particular vitamin being overdosed.

Dr. Berger also points out that individual requirements and tolerances vary—another reason it's imperative to get sound information about supplemental vitamins. Details about proper doses and side effects of overdoses are given in Dr. Berger's book.[8]

TUNING BODY AND MIND WITH EXERCISE

It's no surprise to anyone past forty that our physical performance levels decrease as we get older. We no longer have the endurance and quickness of earlier years. But to some extent, knowledge and experience help us to compensate for the biological decline. This is especially true in sports activities.

The good news is that we can literally retard the aging process with well-chosen exercise. (The more we use what we have, the less we lose.) The right kind of exercise tones and strengthens muscles and maintains and enhances the function of lungs, heart, and other vital organs. Even the brain works better with the increased blood/oxygen flow. Those who opt for a sedentary life may find themselves too soon old, too late smart. As one seventy-five-year-old said, "If I had known I was going to live this long, I would have taken better care of myself."

A word of caution about competitive sports. I am not advocating that you fall into the trap of physical competition with younger persons or trying to outperform your own younger self. Not only is that dangerous, but there are many more appropriate and rewarding goals that you can pursue which will use more of your brain than your brawn.

My enthusiasm for physical exercise during middle and later years presupposes that you will have a thorough physical examination and consult with your physician about the appropriateness, for you, of the different kinds of exercise. Then, given an OK, do it with vigor and enthusiasm. If you are anything like my friends and I, you will experience new feelings of well-being and an enhanced zest for living.

Most experts agree that two of the best exercises for maintaining good health are swimming and walking. However, people of middle and advanced years have enjoyed all kinds of exercise from aerobics to skiing. Some of them golf, some play racquetball, some tennis.

I am a jogger, but that doesn't mean that I advocate jogging for everyone. Eric, a forty-year-old friend, tried it, had serious problems with joints and tendons and gave it up.

Choose something you enjoy and that is appropriate for your particular physical condition. Do it regularly and with a modicum of common sense. Vigorous exercise three times a week will keep you in quite good condition, but four to five times is even better. And it doesn't have to be the same kind of exercise each day. To maintain enthusiasm, get some variety.

Since regularity is important, another question is what exercises or sports can you do alone? For tennis, you need someone on the other side of the net. So even if that is your favorite exercise, you should choose something else to fill in when your favorite antagonist is unavailable.

Thanks to modern machinery, you also have the option of exercising in the comfort, safety, and privacy of your own home. Two popular exercise machines are the stationary bicycle and the rowing machine, the best of which perform admirably with a little sweat on your part. The variety of other exercise devices on the market would be the envy of the keeper of a fourteenth-century torture chamber.

Do you have a physical condition that either temporarily or permanently precludes engaging in your favorite sport? Think before you answer that one.

Dana lost her leg from above the knee to cancer. She skis. In fact, she teaches skiing to others who are handicapped. John plays basketball from a wheelchair as do a whole slew of his friends. There are one-armed baseball players.

The temporary conditions are another matter. Such things as muscle cramps, inflamed joints, tennis elbow, back problems, tendonitis—the things that may call for temporary layoff or special exercises for a time. Don't ignore the symptoms as some people have; some of them didn't even live to regret it. In spite of frustration, do what is necessary to clear them up. We are fortunate today that even some heart conditions can be cleared up with proper treatment.

The younger you start the better. Not only from the standpoint of keeping your body in shape, but also if the activity requires a certain amount of skill, you can more easily develop that skill when you are younger.

THE GOOD NEWS OF MENTAL HEALTH

Earlier in this chapter, I dwelt at some length on the connection between our mental and physical states. Now let's consider a few more thoughts about mental wholeness.

Older persons sometimes hold a frightening vision of themselves becoming mentally incompetent. It's easy for someone worried about such an eventuality to find symptoms where there may be none. If they fail to grasp an idea as quickly as they think they should, or their memory, especially for recent events, has become a bit foggy, they worry that they are irreversibly slipping. But even if their perception of these symptoms is accurate, the cause is usually that they simply are not using their minds actively enough.

There is no scientific evidence that age makes basket cases of us. Many people remain highly productive into their nineties. Of course, just as there are diseases that are common to children, there are diseases that occur among older people and some of these affect the mind.

Progress is being made in understanding the kind of brain atrophy known as Alzheimer's disease which usually strikes people over sixty-five. Because of promising research on this condition, by the time you fifty-year-olds are sixty-five, it may be controllable. Any kind of mental impairment due to some type of dysfunction is a matter for medical attention and will not be further discussed here. Instead, we will turn our attention to those mental health factors that are within our own power to affect.

Just as with physical skills which are not used, mental skills are often lost if we allow them to go unused. Take memory for example (the primary subject of the jokes passed around in senior citizen circles). It's wonderful to have a good sense of humor. But perhaps one of the most important things we tend to forget is how the memory works. Two of the most important factors affecting our memory performance are intention and exercise.

What are those things you really intend to remember? You will remember best those things to which you attach great importance; in other words, those things which you really want to remember tend to stay with you. Things that you aren't interested in just don't register.

And how much do you really exercise your memory; or for that matter your other mental faculties? Taking academic courses is one of the best ways I know to exercise your mind and keep it sharp. In addition to their regular daytime curricula, most high schools and colleges operate extension programs that provide evening classes. Opportunities abound. And, of course, if you have the initiative and determination, you can read and study on your own.

Dr. Graendorf makes my day (and case) when he quotes expert on aging, K. Warner Schaie who challenges the over-fifty person with this picture:

> If you keep your health and engage your mind with the problems and activities of the world around you, chances are good that you will experience little if any decline in intellectual performance in your lifetime. That's the promise of research in the area of adult intelligence.[9]

Schaie's words about memory are just as encouraging:

> . . . very little decline in the ability to learn and remember until very late in life. . . . Motivation is perhaps the key variable in adult education. . . . for old dogs rarely have difficulty learning new tricks; they more often have difficulty convincing themselves that a bone is worth the effort.[10]

To maintain either mental health or physical health, it takes desire and effort. I've been sick and I've been well and, believe me, well is better. Good health at any age is worth the effort.

CHAPTER TEN

FLAVOR LIFE WITH QUALITY LEISURE

Two years ago I shared with our oldest daughter some of my feelings about retirement. She was very patient and attentive. After listening for a while she said, "Dad I think you feel more comfortable in a structured environment. Maybe you should go back to work."

Obvious to her. Shocking to me. I hadn't really thought about it in those terms before. But yes, I had to admit it; at that time, it was true. And why shouldn't it be? I had spent forty years in a structured environment—three and a half years in the Air Force, then college, then working for large companies. I was used to the eight to five grind plus commuting time, the sometimes-longer hours, deadlines, even taking classes in my spare time.

When I relaxed, I felt guilty.

Some of us have spent our whole lives thinking of idleness as a vice. Now when we are either idle or have the opportunity to be idle, how can we help but feel guilty? True, it is false guilt. But our feelings don't know the difference between real guilt and false guilt. Either one is as hard to get rid of as an unreachable itch.

CHALLENGING THE WORK ETHIC

Most of us were trained for work and not for leisure. We were taught the superior importance of work, to feel ashamed of doing nothing while others worked. Duty was of supreme importance. And the fulfillment of our duty conferred a certain dignity upon us. Leisure was looked upon as either the reward of industry or a concession to man's guilty passions. In the Protestant ethic, all enjoyment was suspect.

The work ethic has been used, abused, and misconstrued in many ways. Originated centuries ago as a means of survival, it was later touted as the road to great achievement and success. Now many people have been sidetracked into the mindless pursuit of unnecessary wealth. Even in the small towns the prevalent attitude is to work hard today and save, then tomorrow you can take your ease and enjoy the fruit of your labor.

It is implied that today is for working and tomorrow is for enjoying. Future-itis—a disease that destroys our joy in the present. In the words of Dr. Paul Tournier, "Many people spend their entire life indefinitely preparing to live."[1]

Why is it that many of us have not learned to enjoy creative quality leisure? Is it the old work ethic? Love of vocation? Greed? A desire to keep up with friends and neighbors? Envy of someone else's success? Is it our distorted sense of values? Is it that we can't rid ourselves of a false guilt if we indulge in leisure while others work? Is it simply habit—the eight to five syndrome? Or is it all of the above?

But more important, if we conclude that there is good reason to learn to enjoy creative, quality leisure, how do we break the old chains?

Lest you think that I'm about to launch into a tirade against working, please let me ease your concern regarding that perception. A life of nothing but leisure is not the answer. Many people have found that all play can be as much of a drag as all work.

During my adult life, working seemed more natural than playing. I always envied the guy in the cartoon with the caption "I'm not afraid of hard work. I can lie down right beside it and go to sleep." Only in the last few years have I learned, all over again, how to play. But if you ask my wife, she will tell you I still have a lot to learn.

I've always thought that work was great. But I don't think that work is something to be worshiped. Alone, it isn't the real essence of the good life—the complete, fulfilling, joyful life. Most people need both work and leisure for quality living.

Granted, people are different. Some of our heroes and great achievers were obsessed with and driven by their work. And mankind benefited from their obsession. Situations are different, too. Some of these obsessives didn't have families, at least not for long. Some were geniuses, some recluses, and some eccentrics, with few if any friends.

If you get more satisfaction out of work than anything else maybe you should just forget the pleasure of leisure. But if you do nothing but work, you are, and will continue to be, sacrificing some other things. You are the one who must decide whether your obsession with work is worth the price. Please do this. Think about it seriously and consider the consequences as objectively as possible.

MISLED BY HABIT AND A
HYPERACTIVE CONSCIENCE

Many of my friends extol the virtues of golfing. When I retired I hadn't golfed for thirty years. Too busy working. About a year into retirement after many work projects and much wheel spinning, I concluded that if I were ever going to enjoy this wonderful game I would have to get with it.

Brilliant logic.

I'm the type of golfer who disdains simply to "address" the ball. I "threaten" it! My natural, intense (up-tight) approach to life carried over into my golf game. My score climbed like the national debt. When someone told me to "stay loose" I understood what they meant, but for me, wrestling alligators would have been easier. I discovered that it's difficult but not impossible to change old habits and ways of thinking—to stop turning play into work. The good news is that after some lessons and much practice my golf game improved. The bad news is that some of that practice was more work than play.

A retired acquaintance and I were playing golf together when I asked him what he was doing in his retirement. "Nothing but playing golf," he responded. Then with a touch of vehemence, he added, "I've paid my dues."

I've heard those last words often. The defensive tone of his voice and the set of his jaw told me a great deal. His unspoken words were "you probably think I should be doing something more important, but it's my retirement and I will do what I please."

He got no argument from me.

However, I am aware that doing what you please does not necessarily mean that you are happy with what you are doing. It's like the feeling you get when you've told your friends about your nutritious diet and they catch you eating junk food. In this man's case, a feeling of false guilt was reducing the enjoyment he should have felt.

Ridiculous, true. But it's an attitude I have found many times among retirees. We've been framed by past experiences and environment, by the "shoulds" of well-meaning parents and authority figures, by the work ethic, by a misguided conscience, and by who knows what.

NEEDED: A CHANGE IN OUR THINKING

As I write here in my study with the window open, a sudden gust of wind blows the curtain aside and rustles the papers on my desk. The air smells fresh and sweet. I glance out of the window as it starts to rain—a soft summer shower.

I get up from my desk and walk outside on the patio. The oleanders, roses, honeysuckle, and bright green grass are all reaching for the moisture. A robin digs for worms. In the top of the pine tree a mockingbird joyously proclaims the splendor of God's world. Mixed feelings churn through my mind. Joy and regret compete for attention: joy for the beauty, regret for the few times I have fully enjoyed this backyard in the last twenty years.

It's an American tragedy. It has something to do with how we moderns have seduced ourselves into equating self-worth with net worth and the display thereof—big salaries, large homes, country club memberships, expensive boats, exotic vacations, and countless other trappings of material wealth.

Self-esteem is important. The problem is that we forget the other factors in the equation—the nonmaterial, people-oriented values such as loving relationships, quality time together, service to our fellow humans, our relationship to our creator, and appreciation of his beautiful world. I'm sure you can add to the list.

After many years of wrong thinking, the well-worn grooves in our brains are hard to obliterate. But obliterate we must. We need to embrace new thinking and new values. We need to reprogram ourselves for creative quality leisure.

In the delightful book *When I Relax I Feel Guilty,* author Tim Hansel declares:

> To many, the word leisure has an insubstantial sound. It is like smoke through our fingers. It confuses us, and therefore we mistrust it. Picture postcards cast magic glamour over places to go and things to do, but the nature and essence of true leisure still eludes us. Often this confusion makes us turn leisure into work. Motivated by a false sense of guilt, we transform what should be a joyous weekend release into a Monday morning exhaustion. We turn pleasurable games into hard-fought contests.[2]

Sometimes during our working years, we forget the true meaning and purpose of leisure—the *re-creation* factor. We need to understand the values of both work and leisure and to enjoy both. Each adds a measure of pleasure to the other. And whether in our working years or later, we must learn to redirect our lives toward the guiltless enjoyment of truly creative, quality leisure.

UNINHIBITED DELIGHT

When an adult sees a bug, his inclination is to step on it. A small child seeing a bug will often pick it up to examine it with wide-eyed curiosity, and maybe even taste it.

The song of a mockingbird, a creek-borne family of young ducklings, a sunset, fog cascading over the mountains like slow motion surf, the smell of grass and trees after a rain—these and countless other wonders of God's world are some of my favorite things.

Yet somewhere between Cub Scouts and my first paycheck, I lost some of the capacity to truly enjoy. Quietly, little by little, insidiously, my mind was captured by the pressures of living. My fun-loving spirit, hostage of redirected attention and energy, became as insensitive as a frozen finger. It's a common disease. The good news is it's curable.

Young children have an insatiable sense of wonder at the world; and when they play, it is with their whole being, completely and joyfully absorbed in a delightful happening.

One warm spring day, while their mother went on a shopping trip to San Francisco, our two grandsons, ages five and seven, were left with Alice and me. After spending a delightful hour with them in a nearby park, we walked home and ate lunch. Then I took a nap while the two boys volunteered to help grandma with her gardening. They were assigned the job of watering with a hose.

Of course, anyone could predict the next episode. They began squirting each other with the hose. Noisy emotions threatened a conflict. Grandma Alice was equal to the challenge. She escorted them to a large mound of topsoil at the side of the house and suggested they water that, knowing exactly what would happen next. I woke up from my nap to the sound of the most uninhibited giggles and belly laughs I've ever heard.

Walking cautiously around the house I surveyed the scene. Two boys fully clothed except for shoes were in the middle of a sea of mud, squishing the black stuff between their toes and enthusiastically plastering each other from head to toe with mud. When they paused in the plastering operation, they picked up gobs of mud and threw them at the wooden fence. Each action was accompanied by outrageous giggles. In such a situation, whether parent or grandparent, you have a choice—cry, explode, or laugh. We chose to laugh.

As the giggles began to taper off, Alice took the water hose and washed off the bigger chunks of mud. Then the clothes were stuffed in the washing machine and the boys in the bathtub. Thanks to modern appliances, by the time their mother came home, boys and clothes were clean and dry and the boys were quietly playing something else.

They will never forget that event. And neither will Alice or I.

CREATING NEW THOUGHT PATTERNS

When my logical self says it's stupid not to fully enjoy retirement, my conscience garbles the message. It's as if my logical self is speaking a foreign language my conscience doesn't understand. Occasionally there is a communication breakthrough. That's when the brilliant colors of pure enjoyment fall into beautiful patterns like a kaleidoscope.

The dividing line that distinguishes between work and play is fuzzy. The labels themselves are deceptive. All afternoon here at my desk, I have been absorbed in my writing, thoroughly enjoying it. Is it work or play? Or how about the golfing practice? That may be more work than play.

It all depends on my own perception. It doesn't matter what

someone else thinks it is. In fact, outside observers will disagree on whether it is work or leisure. If I'm enjoying it, with no guilt feelings, satisfied in my own mind that it is a worthwhile expenditure of effort and time, the label doesn't matter.

True, quality leisure is not idleness. It may include idleness, but more often it is activity—some self-chosen activity that you deeply enjoy. Quality leisure is best described as an attitude of the mind.

Now consider this. Alice and I have a very important engagement this evening. We are taking our son and daughter-in-law to dinner. In my mind, that is pure pleasurable play. To someone who has a poor relationship with their daughter-in-law, it might seem more like work.

Would I let my writing interfere with our dinner date? No way. Purged from my vocabulary are the words *deadline, should, have to,* and *not enough time.*

There is no such thing as lack of time. There is more than enough time to do what we want to do. But we may have to adjust our priorities, fine tune our sense of values, and do a better job of time management.

RETHINKING PRIORITIES AND VALUES

We need to re-examine our personal philosophy of work and leisure. For many people work alone is inadequate for fulfillment and quality living. It does not give full expression to their identity, their freedom, and their self-esteem.

It's not that work is bad and leisure is good or the other way around. For a fulfilling life, we need both. To view them in the proper perspective and relationship is the trick. We have the option to change our emphasis between work and play from time to time. But in so doing we need to consider the wishes and welfare of those significant others who are near and dear to us.

If you choose to work, it can be on your own terms—the right days and hours. You can work for a period and then go on a dinner date or take a long trip. You can accept just as much responsibility as you choose. You have the option to say no. But just as important, when some really exciting opportunity comes along, you have the option to say yes.

Set up goals and priorities which include both your work and leisure. You will be amazed at how you can manage to do everything that is worthwhile. Some of the wheel-spinning nitty-gritty may have to be eliminated. If you do this systematically it puts you in charge. Then do first things first.

At those times when you decide in favor of leisure, is it wholehearted, forget-everything-else guiltless enjoyment? How do you feel when you choose work?

Our thorough enjoyment of either work or play depends on being able to purge our minds of a false sense of guilt. Regardless of our choice, to work or play, feeling guilty about it would be like inviting ants to a picnic.

Begin now to sharpen your "sense-abilities" and renew your pleasure in the world God created. Learning to smell the flowers is easier and sweeter when your olfactory sense is in its prime. Make plans to do some of those things you've always wanted to do. Strike your own comfortable balance between work and leisure.

And bear in mind there is an old rabbinic saying that a man will have to give an account on the judgment day for every good thing which he might have enjoyed, and did not.

CHAPTER ELEVEN

KEEPING YOUR MARRIAGE ALIVE

Cliff's wife Helen was still working when he retired. One day she came home, walked in the doorway, and exploded in anger. Without consulting her, Cliff had rearranged the living room furniture. Lamp cords no longer reached the electric wall plugs. Chairs and sofa interfered with operation of drapes. And the worn spot in the carpet, previously covered with the sofa, was now exposed for the whole world to see. The nerve of some husbands.

Cliff discovered he had married a tigress. The furniture was returned to its former location, and Cliff felt fortunate to have escaped with his life.

Sometimes the husband's retirement places a lot of stress on his wife. One wife put it succinctly, "Too little money, too much husband." Perfectly healthy wives have been known to develop hypochondria because of antagonism and frustration.

At retirement the mutual stress on husband and wife can rend their relationship.

> How well can you and your spouse endure each other twenty-four hours a day, seven days a week? Are you adaptable enough to adjust?

How will you cope with inevitable stress?

Is your retirement plan flexible enough to adjust to role changes?

Have you thought about how your relationship may be affected? Are you prepared to work together toward a more deeply satisfying relationship within the context of the retirement scenario?

ROLES AND CONFLICTS IN THE MARRIAGE ARENA

Throughout our lives, almost without realizing it our roles have been changing. For men, the usual family role changes are son to suitor to husband to father to grandfather. Women, of course, have similar role changes—daughter, sweetheart, wife, mother, grandmother. But beyond that, in recent years both men and women are taking on roles that previously were considered the domain of the opposite sex.

When Jerry retired from his own business, his wife Emily continued to work. For two years until Emily retired, Jerry happily played the role of a "house husband." He had no problem with that.

Both Jerry and Emily attribute their harmonious role interchange to early planning and mental preparation. For several years before retirement they took self-improvement courses relating to attitudes, values, and interpersonal communication— not specifically for retirement, but rather as an enhancement of life quality. The help in retirement adjustment was incidental but effective. No doubt, other factors such as Jerry's and Emily's personalities played a part in their satisfactory adaptation.

There is no simple standard pattern in the way people adapt. It depends on personality, ego, self-image—a host of psychological factors which make up the total self.

I would have had a problem with being a house husband.

And so would some others I know. Fortunately, Alice retired before I did, so I was never confronted with that particular problem. But I did have problems associated with finding a new identity. Alternating between loving concern and exasperation, Alice could do nothing to help me through the maze. The resulting frustration put a lot of stress on her and on our relationship. For a time, her blood pressure actually went up twenty points. Then when I finally got my act together, it promptly shrank back to normal.

Steve, a retired airline pilot who had an identity crisis, resented his role change. His frustration and resentment carried over into his relationship with his wife, Evelyn. Wagging his head as he followed her around the house, he displayed all the symptoms of the "Friendly Puppy Syndrome." "I could have lived with him watching me work except for one thing," she said. "Every now and then he would ask me, 'Why are you doing it that way?' I came within a cobweb of wrapping the dust mop around his neck."

Having a discontented Steve underfoot loaded Evelyn with stress. She had developed many outside interests over the years while Steve was working and had a carefully planned day-to-day agenda. Now that was all being shredded by her concern and efforts to help Steve.

As a result, Evelyn suffered both mental and physical problems, which is not at all unusual in the process of adjusting to retirement. The good news is that Steve and Evelyn were able to work out their problems, but only after Steve began some projects he felt were important—projects that challenged his mind and skills.

An identity crisis is often brought on by a role change. The new role becomes the person's new identity. If that identity is not acceptable to the person's self-image, inner conflict develops and must be resolved before the person can be happy.

This inner conflict erupts in many ways such as personality changes, poor attitudes, hypochondria, male impotence, and a chip on the shoulder. Any or all of these can impose great stress on both the spouse and the retiree and devastate their relationship.

THE MARRIAGE RELATIONSHIP—
A TWO-RING CIRCUS

Marriages go through phases. Each marriage relationship changes with time, circumstances, and growth (or lack thereof) of the partners. Generally, dividing lines are fuzzy and the phases blend together rather than change abruptly. Also the phase characteristics and how they progress from one to the other vary with the marriage.

As I explain the diagram in figure 11.1 you will see that the life cycle of most marriages closely resembles this model. The overlapping Husband/Wife areas signify the partners' degree of involvement in their marriage relationship. The ratios of the different areas will, of course, vary from marriage to marriage, but the concept of changing involvement is still applicable.

In Phase 1, early marriage, the partners are eager and able to supply most of each other's needs. Although some needs are still supplied outside the marriage, the lovers are deeply involved with each other.

Phase 2 represents a later time which includes the years of child-raising and career-building—more or less mid life, say the ages between thirty and fifty. A busy phase when husband and wife find too little time to spend together as a couple. Raising a family, working hard in their career(s), taking on outside activities in community or church, possibly the responsibility of elderly parents. They all add up to "whew!"

"Time to talk to Kathy?" Ralph asked. "Are you kidding? I come home and find this stranger in my house, and she tells me she's my wife. But I'm not really sure. Maybe I can find out two

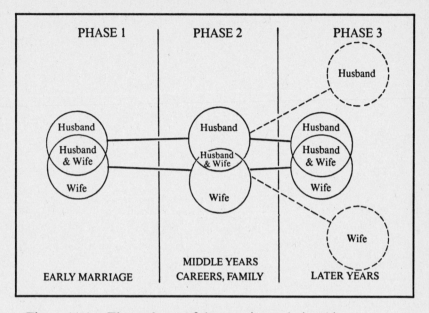

Figure 11.1.   Three phases of the marriage relationship.

months from now when I take this 'stranger' on my vacation."

In Phase 2, there is often a certain amount of growing away from each other. At this stage, it seems as though everyone is pushing your buttons. Individual demands on both of you reduce time and opportunity for involvement with each other as a couple. This is represented in the diagram by a smaller Husband/ Wife area. A marriage or remarriage after mid life usually skips Phase 2.

Phase 3 comes after the children are gone and careers have peaked; this is roughly ages fifty and up. The dotted lines in this part of the diagram represent the situation where the partners have become married singles, little or no mutual involvement, and finally decide to dissolve the marriage. The solid lines represent a healthy marriage in which the partners rediscover each other and, once again, become aware of each other's feelings and renew and revitalize their deep loving relationship. They are in a position to say no to button pushers, outsiders who make demands on them, and to take time to replenish their own emotional reserves.

RETIREMENT ALTERS THE RELATIONSHIP

The very simplicity of the diagram in figure 11.1 disguises the bumpy road people often travel from Phase 2 to Phase 3 via the solid lines. Except for the pain, the dashed lines are easy. Just ignore your spouse and you arrive there with no effort. If you want to go the route of the solid lines, read on.

People who have lived together through the many years of Phase 2 have, either consciously or unconsciously, worked out a satisfactory way of relating and working together. Each partner has accepted certain functions and responsibilities, and each one has come to depend on his/her spouse to competently perform as expected. As situations require it, they may switch roles or temporarily take on a responsibility normally performed by the other spouse.

Over the years, circumstances change, and as they adapt themselves to those changes, so does their lifestyle. Children may leave home or the wife may begin a new career outside the home. But these periodic changes usually do not prevent most marriage relationships from running as reliably as a well-maintained auto—that is, as long as each one continues to perform his or her role. Some tender loving care and a few repairs along the way usually get these couples over the bone-bruising, bumpy road of middle life without any catastrophic breakdowns.

But now what? No matter how well you know each other or how much rough road you have shared, marriage before retirement does little to prepare you for marriage after retirement. It can be as traumatic as the reputed mid-life crisis.

The changes are significant and abrupt—surprises. You can't anticipate everything. You and your spouse are suddenly spending a lot more time together. Old habits, r)les, routines, schedules, responsibilities, and relationships are revised, reversed, disturbed, or confused.

Strange habits and traits are exposed—things like obsessive neatness, petulant response to frustration, anxiety for no good reason, hypochondria, poor attitudes. Anyone who has traversed the valley can name others.

You are bewildered. Things have changed. And you don't like change in something that has been very satisfactory. But suddenly the gears are clashing and the machine is clanking instead of purring. Not understanding the why and the how of it, you are confused and disoriented by the suddenness of it all. Something must be done before the machine blows up.

It's enough to make a woman think she kissed the wrong frog. Sometimes she entertains the idea of finding another one: a frog that has a more melodious croak and catches bigger bugs.

In a relationship which appears to be operating smoothly before retirement, the sudden discord befuddles both men and women. When George retired, he visualized freedom—freedom to do impulsive things with his wife Adele, to take off for either short or long trips, attend plays or symphonies in the city, drive to their cabin for several days of fishing, or visit their children and grandchildren. They could do their traveling on weekdays and avoid the weekend traffic. It sounded great and George couldn't understand why Adele objected to dropping her activities on short notice to go with him.

During the years when George was preoccupied with his work, Adele had filled the empty spaces of her life with social affairs and volunteer work which occupied most weekdays. She didn't want to back out of her commitments. But it wasn't just that, she enjoyed these activities and was reluctant to dismantle her agenda. She was so busy that George almost had to get an appointment to talk to her. And when they did discuss the problem, her attitude was that she wasn't busy every day and why didn't he find something else to do on those days when she was occupied with other things. But George hadn't expected this situation, and he refused to revise his dream.

Frustrated, George sulked and considered his options: taking a cruise by himself, becoming a hermit, looking for a kissing princess, or going back to work. He couldn't think of any really challenging project that he would be willing to devote himself to. So George went back to work, utterly disillusioned by his short retirement.

Now George tells me that at last he and Adele are beginning to talk about the problems and perhaps in a year or two they can both compromise and build a dream retirement that they can enjoy together.

We are our own worst enemy. Our natural inertia, a reluctance to accept the need for change and resistance to modifying old routines, sometimes results in passing the point of no return—a blown relationship.

Some adjustments are absolutely necessary. And they are much less painful and easier to negotiate if a couple is aware of possible problems and is willing to talk about them before retirement. A communication gap can devastate a marriage.

MODERN MARRIAGE CRISIS

» Don and Mabel «

The early darkness didn't matter much to Don as he threaded his way through the dimly lighted parking lot. November was not his favorite month, but the long hours of overtime blended the months together so he was scarcely aware of the seasons.

As he eased his old Chevy into the traffic, his headlights shone back at him from the shiny bumper of the car in front. Bumper to bumper, slow and go. He might as well relax; it would be another forty minutes before he triggered the garage-door opener.

The steady hum of the heater fan and the soft comfort of the car seat lulled him into a semi-dream state. His mind began flipping through the pages of his life. Now forty-seven, he had been married to Mabel for twenty-three years, definitely a love match. One of their sons was a fledgling engineer, one a salesman, and their daughter was a freshman in college.

Proud of what he had accomplished, Don reminisced about how well he had taken care of his family, especially Mabel. Six years ago they moved into a new house in a beautiful neighborhood. Then five years ago he bought the baby grand piano that Mabel had always wanted. Last year when their second son had become independent, Don gave her a new Mercedes and told her she could buy anything she wanted. It was strange though; she seemed to hardly hear him.

Don was conscientious about sending Mabel a dozen roses for anniversaries. On her birthday he took her to that exotic new restaurant. He smiled in remembering. Then the smile faded as he thought about hurrying through their dessert so he could return to the office to prepare for the next day's sales meeting.

Oh, they didn't spend a lot of time together. After all, Mabel was doing her thing with her part-time job and her bridge luncheons. Oh yes, and then there was that society she belonged to. Let's see, what was the name of it? He was surprised at his lack of recall. No matter. It had something to do with community service. Whatever it was, she seemed to enjoy it.

What was it Mabel had said about Hawaii? Something about wanting to go there for their anniversary. But she must understand that long hours and business crises limited vacations to catch as catch can. They would go sometime.

He was suddenly disturbed by another flash of meddlesome memory. It was about two weeks ago right after dinner. He was reading the business news, delving into the prospect of higher interest rates. Not even half listening, he did remember her saying something about her job. What was it anyway? Something to do with going to college to qualify for another position. That meddlesome memory of his. If it was going to remember anything, why couldn't it remember all the details? Maybe he should ask her about it.

As he swung the car into the driveway he thrust a finger at the garage door opener and drew to a smooth stop in the cluttered garage. Grabbing his briefcase, he strode quickly into the house, closing the garage door behind him.

Mabel was not in the kitchen, but Don knew she must be around somewhere. Her car was in the garage. His call elicited a perfunctory "in the living room" from his wife.

Late again, Don ate his cold dinner alone. Nothing unusual about that. He didn't notice that Mabel was quieter than usual. She made no attempt to talk to him. When he walked into the living room on his way to his study, she looked up from her book and gave him an expressionless "hi." He pecked her on the cheek and asked "What's new?" Her answer of "nothing" seemed to have a note of finality about it.

In his study, he was soon absorbed in his work, yet disturbed when his mind kept returning to his wife. He finally dismissed it as a quirk of fatigue, and went to bed. In his deep sleep he never knew when or whether Mabel came to bed.

At breakfast the next morning, when Mabel tried to start a conversation, Don only emitted a grunt or two from behind his newspaper. Suddenly a strange note in her voice jolted him.

He dropped his paper and looked up as Mabel, half sobbing, said, "I want a divorce."

SHARING THOUGHTS AND FEELINGS

Don and Mabel's communication gap was like a collapsed bridge that plunged them into a whirlpool of misunderstanding.

Divorced people attribute the dissolution of their marriage to many things: incompatibility, growing apart, money, diverging interests, infidelity, adultery, and cruelty. You've heard them all. However, these things are often only symptoms of a more basic cause. The fabric of most sick marriages has been weakened by one flimsy thread: poor communication between the partners. Like so many others, Don and Mabel's marriage needed mouth-to-ear resuscitation.

It seems we're better at getting married than staying married. As Dr. Allan Fromme said so succinctly, "Sharing a roof over one's head or even the same bed isn't enough to keep people close, and certainly not enough to bring them closer. There must be constant sharing of thought and feeling with mutual respect."[1]

When the kids were home, Don and Mabel seemed to have more to talk about. Now it seemed to Mabel that, whenever she tried to talk to him, his mind was somewhere else. Competing with his career, urgent meetings, the newspaper, and his computer made her feel like a nonperson. Don's computer knew him better than Mabel did. He was so preoccupied with his career that he didn't even realize what was going on until the sky fell.

Mabel was wandering in an emotional desert, starved for understanding—lonely and frustrated. She wanted to talk with Don about important things; to share thoughts and feelings about the good times and the bad times, the frustrations and triumphs. For a few hours of this kind of communication, she would gladly have given up her new Mercedes.

Instead of listening carefully to Mabel's messages, Don was playing and listening to his own tapes. He considered himself a good husband. After all he was giving Mabel everything that a cherished wife could want. Or so he thought. In reality, he was giving her what he fantasized she would enjoy, which was not bad as far as it went. But the all-important gifts—listening and sharing—were missing.

Mabel wanted to reach a deeper understanding of the man she loved, and to be understood by him. If he was angry, she needed to know why. Was it her fault? Was it the aggressive driver that beat the red light and forced him to slam on his brakes and lay down thirty feet of skid marks? Was it his unreasonable boss who gave him an impossible deadline? Was it the newspaper headlines about the deteriorating economy?

Since Don didn't reveal either his feelings or their source, Mabel often blamed herself. And this false guilt was eating her up. I can hear women readers saying, "So what's new?" In a survey conducted by the *Ladies Home Journal* in which 104,000 women responded, 36 percent complained that their husbands don't share their feelings.[2]

Lest you think I'm being too hard on the men on this subject, I hasten to say that some women are as reluctant as men to talk about thoughts and feelings. And that will mangle a marriage just as much as an uncommunicative husband.

The point is that many of the marriage mountains can be reduced to molehills by being willing to talk about them, to express feelings honestly, to listen to the other person with your mind and heart as well as your ears, and then to accept the other person regardless of the feelings he or she expresses.

MARRIED SINGLES

Some married couples could be classified as married singles. If a marriage is going to be a meaningful relationship it must involve a reasonable amount of both physical and mental togetherness. This does not mean doing everything together. However, it does mean enjoying each other's company so much that you deeply want to share some good times; not only that, but it also means that you love each other deeply enough to want to share the bad times.

I have heard many wives say "I just can't get him to talk to me" or "I can't speak to him about that; he'll just get mad." Some wives, after trying for years, give up. Then they settle for a silent partnership or look for a greener lily pad and a frog with fewer warts.

If it's the wife who won't express her feelings, her husband may feel that he's walking on eggs every time he opens his mouth. He doesn't know how his wife will respond nor what she is thinking or feeling. If this continues, he may begin looking for a kissing princess.

The problem is compounded by the fact that people can actually flap their lips for years without really communicating. Talk is not necessarily communication. Real communication means an accurate and complete understanding of the messages being transmitted by each person—good sending and good receiving, honest verbalizing and careful listening.

All too often, we lean toward small talk and trivia and avoid the real gut issues. We are reluctant to reveal true and sometimes intense feelings because there is a certain amount of risk involved.

We fear conflict and confrontation and the possibility of being rejected. And if we do work up enough courage to let it all hang out, the other person may refuse to accept us or our feelings. So we are often unwilling to take that risk.

No good marriage gets that way by drinking a love potion, buying lottery tickets, or tossing coins in a fountain. If you and your spouse are serious about maintaining and enhancing the quality of your relationship, it takes dedication. Any time you have to overcome your own inertia, as well as navigate troubled, uncharted waters, it takes work.

SOME FRICTION POINTS

As an example of the kind of conflict that may develop in retirement, consider the simple concept of space (territory).

Husbands, your wife is accustomed to being the unchallenged

queen in her territory. It may be the kitchen, garden, her painting studio, or something else. She has been managing these
things successfully for many years. She should not and will not
tolerate a foreign potentate invading her territory and telling her
how to run things. If you think you're a better cook, don't try to
prove it.

And don't be seduced into blunders by the tantalizing idea of
getting your wife better organized. She would be completely
justified in starting a full-scale war with the invader. Or it
might be a cold war—silence during the day and a headache at
night.

Be forewarned. Respect your wife as an individual with certain rights and needs, among which is a territory she can continue to call her own.

Wives, your husband has certain territory where he exercises
his kingly role. His workshop is a shambles with tools, nuts and
bolts, spare parts and scrap lumber scattered randomly over
workbenches and the garage floor. And you could make it so
neat! Or the desk in his study is covered with papers, with other
papers, magazines and books scattered about, even on the floor.
What would guests think if they glanced in there on their way to
the bathroom? It's safer to just shut the door than to rearrange
his treasures.

If you wish to survive longer than the unfortunate wives of
Henry VIII, don't mess with your husband's toys. Hands off
unless you have a personal and specific invitation from him.
Respect him as an individual with certain rights, needs, and
inviolate space.

Of course, these are only samples of the possible areas of
friction. Other sore subjects may be hobbies, sports, clubs, av-
ocations, friends, irritating habits, use of the phone, division of
household chores, and where to go on a vacation. All have been
known to raise the blood pressure from time to time.

Many of these potential problems merely smolder a bit before retirement, and you're not together enough to smell the smoke. After retirement, you are surprised when some of the smoldering embers roar into three-alarm conflagrations. Learning to douse fires before they occur will reduce wear and tear on your emotions.

GETTING IN TOUCH WITH YOUR OWN FEELINGS

The dissonance of conflict is not always audible to the ear. Silent discord can be more disturbing to the mind than clashing cymbals and thundering drums.

Some men (and women) come home after a bad day and kick the dog and yell at their spouse and kids. Some harbor a time-delayed reaction: a tendency to bottle up frustrations inside for long periods of time. Then when they least expect it, the frustrations burst forth in hostility and unreasonable anger triggered by some unrelated "last straw" event. It seldom occurs to them that the explosion was caused by confined pressure that has been building up for a long time.

One of the biggest hurdles in reaching our communication goal is to get in touch with our own feelings. In talking with other people, I have learned that many, like myself, have bottled up their feelings for so long they don't know what they look like. It's only when we pour them out that we can examine and deal with them.

Too often we prefer to live in a no-man's land of hang-ups, disagreements, and forbidden topics. We shudder at the prospect of confrontation. Yet once we learn to express and accept each other's thoughts and feelings without coming unglued, we find that the fire-spouting dragon turns into a warm teddy bear.

There are some techniques that can help you get in touch with your feelings. Not only that, but they go a long way toward resolving some of the problems in marriage relationships.

DIGGING FOR DIAMONDS

Before retirement, many men are bigamists; they're married to a wife and a career. Many wives of such men have become stoic about their marriage. Busy raising children and managing the home or holding down their own job, they elected to accept the situation. When the children left home, these women plunged into other activities to fill the emptiness. The marriage continued to be convenient and met some of their needs. But along the way they learned to satisfy many of their needs outside the marriage relationship. In the togetherness of retirement, continuing that attitude can mangle a marriage.

Most of us, given a choice, would trade a stale marriage for one that is exciting and fulfilling rather than opt for singleness. A vibrant marriage makes life sparkle with all the luster of a perfect diamond. Yet, we don't always realize that we need not venture into new territory to find the diamonds. They are in our own backyard—in the marriage we have. And what are these diamonds? I'll stack them up and dazzle you with their splendor:

> love
> tenderness
> trust
> respect
> joy
> fulfillment

But these diamonds are not just scattered on the surface of your marriage. Finding them takes work—digging. There may be mountains of misunderstanding that must be moved by developing the art of communication. But whatever the mountains, before you begin excavating, prepare your mind with:

▸ A realization that retirement will strain your relationship.

▸ A belief that something can be done about it before retirement.

▶ A strong desire on the part of you and your spouse to make your marriage the best it can be.

▶ An open mind willing to dig something besides ruts, and willing to forego judgment as to who is the hero and who is the villain.

In marriage enrichment, even the digging is fun. And the discovery much more so. It's time now to learn how to dig those diamonds for a rich and vibrant marriage.

CHAPTER TWELVE

STRATEGY FOR A VIBRANT MARRIAGE

If medals and campaign ribbons were awarded for the battles, campaigns, and crises that the normal marriage goes through, by mid life some married couples would have their chests full. But there are no purple hearts with clusters for the wounds sustained in these experiences—not even "hazard" pay.

Some years ago, Alice and I had invited our friends Karen and Larry to our house for the evening. The oldest of their six children (four boys and two girls) was fifteen, and he and the next oldest were baby-sitting the younger four in their home.

We two couples were in a very relaxed mood and having a wonderful time time reveling in our friendship. As gales of laughter bounced off the walls our twelve-year-old daughter walked in. For a moment she stood in the living room doorway until she could be heard. Then she said, "I love to hear you laugh like that. You should do it more often."

The room was suddenly quiet as Karen said, "Raising six kids is no laughing matter."

Recently we enjoyed another visit with Karen and Larry and recalled some of the events of the intervening twenty years. With experiences that ranged from Cub Scouts and Girl Scouts to an accident that cost one boy a leg, from a college basketball star to rebellious teen-agers, from hippies to straights, from children finding themselves and succeeding to one son's broken marriage, they had laughed and cried their way through the triumphs and disappointments of parenthood.

Now Larry has retired from his long-time career, and he and Karen have started a clothing store. Life's battles have drawn them closer together and, although working hard, they are living some vintage years. Theirs is a deep, loving relationship.

Not so with Tom and Nancy. Over the years, they had fewer problems than Karen and Larry. But when their four kids had flown the nest, they discovered that their communications were garbled. They were broadcasting on different wave lengths. It seemed that for twenty-five years their only common interest was raising their kids. Now without those connecting threads, their marriage fabric rotted and split.

Not all marriages are created equal. There are, for various reasons, good ones and bad ones. What makes the difference between a marriage that is just barely breathing on its own and one that is vigorous, exciting, and fulfilling?

MARRIAGE ENRICHMENT

In the words of marriage counselors David and Vera Mace, *"We can have better marriages if we really want them."*[1] A couple can discover a higher level of satisfaction through a marriage enrichment program.

Although marriage enrichment usually includes sweet words and erotic glances, it goes much deeper than that. It is a commitment to love that grows from within the relationship when two people work at it. It is growing closer through a deeper understanding of each other. All of which is enabled by learning how to really communicate with each other in a loving, constructive way.

The first key to a better marriage is desire. The second is an open mind.

Searching for better communication, Alice and I stumbled through dry deserts, over rocky mountains, and down the dark alleys of misunderstanding. We attended classes in communication skills, and we sincerely tried to practice what we learned. At first we were so clumsy that when we tried some of the techniques on our kids, they got a funny look in their eyes and asked, "Why are you acting so weird?"

We made progress. But it wasn't until we went on a special weekend retreat called Marriage Encounter (ME) that a whole new world opened up. We were both fifty-four years old at the time. Some of the couples were older, some much younger. In that short weekend, we discovered more about ourselves and our relationship than we had learned in our previous thirty years of marriage.

You don't believe it? Just try it. There are thousands of couples all over the country who have had the experience and would welcome an opportunity to prove to you that I'm right.

Caution. Marriage Encounter is not magic. It teaches you how to nourish your marriage relationship. It is not for marriages that are already crashing on the rocks. ME will make a good marriage better, but once the ship is breaking up, you need professional help in the form of marriage counseling to put it back together.

Furthermore, ME does not eliminate the wrinkles that appear from time to time in the fabric of your marriage. But it does teach you how to iron out the wrinkles without burning the material.

But I'm getting ahead of myself.

Just what is Marriage Encounter?

In simple terms, it is an extremely practical program to teach couples a technique of communication—how to share thoughts and feelings in a way that cements the relationship in a stronger bond of love. It doesn't end with the weekend. The participants take it home and practice it on a regular basis. Many who have become friends with other couples on the weekend continue to meet together and support each other with weekly or bi-weekly meetings. Often out of this experience, the couples build warm and inspiring friendships.

Marriage Encounter is not a therapy program nor is it group dynamics. It does not involve relating to other people. What happens, happens just between you and your spouse. Each couple rediscovers each other in a deeper way through the method taught and shared on the weekend. It helps you to get in touch with your own feelings so that you can understand both yourself and your spouse and share that understanding with each other. Followed sincerely, the techniques learned in Marriage Encounter have the potential to make any marriage better.

In his book *The Marriage Encounter,* Chuck Gallagher quotes one couple describing its impact:

> This method allows people to reveal themselves to each other in a most loving and honest way. It gives them an opportunity to set aside fears and affirm their mutual love in a very tangible, believable way. It gives them an opportunity to receive and accept love.[2]

I recommend that you read Chuck Gallagher's book which tells you what ME is about. Then sign up and go on a weekend. Many different church denominations are associated with ME and some churches have programs for marriage renewal similar to ME.

Your appetite whetted, find some couples who have experienced a ME weekend and talk to them. Their living example, the closeness, warmth, and joy you observe in these couples will convince you it's not a mirage. If these people were your friends before their experience, you will notice an attractive change.

If your marriage is on the brink of a breakup, Marriage Encounter is probably not for you. You would be better served by counseling. Dr. Mace calls it "training"; teaching couples new methods of interacting with each other so that they can attain their relationship goals.[3]

Churches often have good trained counselors, but if your church doesn't have such a person on its staff, the minister can probably recommend a good marriage counselor. Before you make a commitment to a counselor, interview him/her to find out about their philosophy and attitudes toward marriage. Will his values and yours be a reasonable match?

TACKLING SENSITIVE SUBJECTS

Dave was accustomed to having his wife cheerfully prepare his lunch when he was employed full time at his pre-retirement job. When he retired, he spent much of his time golfing and doing a few odd jobs around the house and yard. He had plenty of time to prepare his own lunch. But human nature and habits being what they are, he expected his wife Joyce to continue preparing his lunch even when she wanted to be away from home during the lunch hour. After several weeks of preliminary sparring, confrontation was inevitable.

One day as Joyce prepared to go shopping, Dave asked her, "Will you fix my lunch before you leave or will you come back home to fix it?"

Without so much as a pause in her exit, Joyce pointedly replied, "Stick it in your ear."

It only took a flip of the lip for Joyce to give him an unmistakable message. They were on the cutting edge of a new relationship.

"How did you feel about that?" I asked Dave.

He chuckled, "I went into shock, but only for a minute. When I recovered, I had to laugh. I said to myself, 'that's my Joyce.' I'm a big boy. My request was really absurd. That evening Joyce and I had a good discussion about our feelings."

Some marriages would have freeze-dried over such an incident, but Dave and Joyce have a healthy relationship. They have learned how to express and accept strong feelings without coming unraveled.

There is nothing unusual or sinister about marriage conflicts. In fact, a certain amount of conflict can be healthy. It all depends on how the partners respond to the conflicts. If they learn, through conflict resolution, how to reveal thoughts and feelings and to accept each other's revelations, it can mean a closer, deeper relationship.

What are the friction points in your own marriage, the sore subjects, the annoying bugs buzzing around in your head?

Write out each one, giving enough detail so that you thoroughly understand what is bugging you, and not only you, but if your spouse were to read the list, she/he would also understand what you mean.

Next and most important, describe as accurately as you can how you feel about each subject. Writing helps you concentrate and really think about it, and finally reach an understanding of how you really feel. This is absolutely essential to reaching amicable resolutions for sore subjects. If you don't know how you feel, how can your spouse ever understand what is bothering you?

Now before you attack your spouse with your list or even reveal that you have one, encourage him/her to make a list.

How?

If your positions were reversed what would sell you on the idea of making such a list?

Feeling that your spouse loves and values you as a person?
Feeling that your spouse is sincerely interested in ironing out a wrinkled relationship?

Whatever you have done in the past to successfully get your spouse in a good mood, do it. And then express a desire to understand everything in your life together that may be causing friction. Above all, make it clear to your spouse that this is not just a sneaky way to criticize or complain but that your marriage is very important to you and you have an honest desire to mutually solve your problems.

Now comes the dialogue. (A little more mood music, please.) Taking the first step to discuss hang-ups and forbidden topics is like stepping out of the airplane on your first parachute jump. It's scary. It's not easy to start a conversation with your spouse on a subject you are quite sure will arouse an earthquake-like response. And what about you? Are you likely to erupt like a verbal volcano when your spouse brings up certain subjects?

I suggest that you let your spouse select the first subject to be discussed. If you and your spouse have already learned how to communicate effectively with each other, congratulations. Use your communication skills to honestly verbalize your feelings and desires. Each of you must be willing to really listen to the other person. Show a sincere interest in what the other person is saying with active listening. Then accept your spouse when he/she is being honest.

If your attempt to discuss these sore subjects goes reasonably well, you're on your way. If it ends in a no-holds-barred battle, you and your spouse may need to fall back and regroup.

Classes in communication are offered in many communities, especially in those having colleges. There are many books available on communication as related to marriage and family, some of which are listed in the bibliography of this book.

SATISFYING NEEDS THROUGH MARRIAGE

What happens to you and your spouse in your marriage relationship depends on what is going on in your two heads, how you communicate these things to each other, and the accompanying attitudes and emotions.

A good marriage is many things. It is fulfilling certain needs of the partners. It is trust and intimate sharing with deep love. It is each spouse granting the other one the right and freedom to develop his/her full potential as a person. Far from stifling the individuals, a good marriage contributes significantly to each person's growth.

There are human needs which are satisfied better by the marriage relationship than by any other lifestyle. Not necessarily in the order of priority, the following needs are those most often listed by married people:

> companionship
> love, affection, sentiment
> sex
> home and family
> a helpmate
> security
> community acceptance

Men and women often list them in different orders of importance, but for our purpose that is irrelevant. The important thing is for husband and wife to understand and accept each other's needs and be willing to meet those needs as far as is reasonably possible.

As we move through the stages of life, our needs change and take on different priorities—reason enough to keep in emotional and intellectual touch with each other through good communication.

THE DEPENDENT WIFE

Is it possible for husband and wife to be dependent on each other and still be independent enough for each to develop his or her full potential as a happy, interesting, and fulfilled person? Are there risks in becoming too dependent?

In the traditional marriage, husband and wife assume the roles of breadwinner and homemaker respectively. Over the years the fine-tuned division of labor that develops, especially where children are raised, is certain to result in interdependency between husband and wife. They perform different but essential roles and seldom trade places. In this set up, each becomes a 'specialist' in his/her particular activity and learns little about the other's role.

This traditional arrangement can, and often does, inhibit the growth of one or both of the partners and can warp the relationship. Bob and Ruth are a case in point.

Ruth was trapped in her husband's attitudes. Several years before Bob planned to retire, Ruth began to worry about finances. She would ask Bob, "Do we have enough money to live on and stay in this house, or will we have to sell and move?" To which macho Bob would reply like a robot-voiced, recorded message, "Don't worry about it. I'll take care of our finances."

That's a put-down for an adult. Ruth continues to worry. Later she confided, "I'm tired of trying to get him to talk about it. He just gets mad."

This attitude occurs not only in the financial area but in others as well. Husbands acting out their role as head of the household often unthinkingly convey a very deprecating message to their wives. That message is, "I don't trust you. I think you are incapable of understanding certain things. I do not need your help to make these important decisions."

It's Stone-Age thinking if Bob really believes this. Ruth is a very intelligent woman with a lot of common sense. If Bob had honestly enlisted Ruth's aid in planning and managing their finances, some blunders could have been avoided. I say this from my own experience. Because I have, in recent years, been willing to listen to my wife, she has prevented my impulsiveness from capsizing our financial ship.

There is another reason a wife needs to know the details about the family's financial affairs. The alligators lurking in the financial swamp feast on those persons who, through ignorance, don't recognize or know how to avoid becoming victims of their scams. The greater a person's knowledge, the safer he/she is.

The reluctance of men to take their wives into their financial confidence has something to do with their masculine ego. And if, like many people in their forties and fifties, they base planning and behavior on an assumption of immortality, they do the surviving spouse a great disservice.

We are seeing exciting changes in men's thinking. Realizing that women are their intellectual equals, many men are sharing responsibilities and ideas that give the marriage a depth they never dreamed possible. I see this more and more, especially with couples in the thirty to forty age bracket where both spouses are working outside the home. The husband may cook dinner while his wife makes out the income taxes. Or the wife does the gardening while her husband entertains the kids.

Such role trading can do a lot for individual and couple growth. And of course, in the event of the temporary absence or the loss of a spouse, the other can carry on without crashing. Just as in making sure both pilot and copilot can fly the airplane, it saves wear and tear on the fear factor.

THE DEPENDENT HUSBAND

Now what about husbands? From my research, it appears that men are at least as likely as women to be discombobulated by the loss of their mate. A husband left to his own devices would have just as many problems as a wife, albeit different ones. Many men in their preoccupation with their career and lack of interest in things domestic have not learned much about taking care of themselves or their children. However, that is changing in the younger generation.

How would you manage without your wife?

Sally, a homemaker, had spent years living within a restricted budget, finding bargains and feeding and clothing her family with good quality and minimum cost. But her husband John, like many of us, didn't appreciate his wife's management talents. When he retired, he talked her into letting him do the food shopping.

Ecstatic with this opportunity to demonstrate his superior financial sagacity, he shopped and shopped and shopped. He drooled over the bargains. Sales and case-lot deals. Incredible opportunities. But he forgot one thing. Unneeded foods are not a bargain. Two months later when Sally had reason to inspect the closet in their guest bedroom, she almost became a Fibber McGee casualty. Case lots stacked from floor to ceiling rocked precariously as she opened the door. But that wasn't all. When confronted, John sheepishly admitted there were more bargains in the cupboard in the garage.

John now knows enough about shopping to do it right next time. And Sally is enjoying greater appreciation from John. But they are not the only people who benefited from that experience. A charitable food kitchen received a donation large enough to feed many needy families for several weeks.

I must admit that I would flounder without my wife. I especially rely on her skills as cook. The last time I tried cooking my own steak, I laid it across the oven grill without a drip pan underneath. What a mess. I gave the fire department a reason for existing. To do my own cooking beyond a bowl of oatmeal, a fried egg, or a hamburger, I would be starting from go. Even though I'm still something of a domestic klutz, I'm learning more all the time.

Alice is also the one who nourishes our friendships and our family relationships much more than I do. Not that I don't enjoy the sociability and closeness of our family. I deeply appreciate these things. But Alice does the promoting: extending and accepting invitations. If she were no longer around, I would not only feel her loss, but also that of some of our friends.

We are adjusting our system. I'm taking my own advice and tuning Alice in on all our financial matters. She is teaching me how to take a more active role in our social and family affairs. Perfection is not just around the corner. The machinery still squeaks, but with a little more loving attention, I'm certain it will begin to purr.

LOVE AND DEPENDENCY

No one has ever arrived at a truly satisfactory, and simple, definition of love. There are so many facets to love that trying to define it in brief simple terms is like trying to adequately describe a tree by the color of its leaves. However, some definitions come close to the essence. One such example is Dr. M. Scott Peck's definition of love as: "The will to extend one's self for the purpose of nurturing one's own or another's spiritual growth."[4]

The very act of extending one's self promotes personal growth. It also implies effort, and an act of the will. Love is not a feeling. It is a decision, a choice.

Dr. Peck points out that dependency is not love. He says:

> When you require another individual for your survival, you are a parasite on that individual. There is no choice, no freedom involved in your relationship. It is a matter of necessity rather than love. Love is the free exercise of choice. Two people love each other only when they are quite capable of living without each other but *choose* to live with each other.[5]

He goes on to define dependency as "the inability to experience wholeness or to function adequately without the certainty that one is being actively cared for by another."[6]

As I have pointed out in previous sections of this chapter, healthy couples will instinctively, sometimes by necessity, switch roles from time to time. It can be fun and stretching and, of course, reduces their mutual dependency. In addition, it is great training for survival in the event of loss of your spouse.

But even more important, the quality of a marriage is greatly enhanced when both spouses are strong and independent.

GROWING TOGETHER AND INDIVIDUALLY

In the later stages of life, the word companionship takes on a new and deeper meaning.

The happiest people are the ones who are sharing their later years in a loving relationship with a compatible companion—each one respecting the other, sharing thoughts and feelings (the good times and the bad), allowing the other to develop his/her full potential.

I realize the kind of growing together I have pictured here is not always possible. But consider the alternatives. Just think of the utter futility of suddenly being an older couple living together with nothing to say to each other. Co-habitation with a stranger or divorce. I shudder.

By age fifty, it's time to put our lives, including our marriage relationship, in total perspective. We're approaching the end of Phase 2. Most careers are peaking. Most women have closed out one successful career, that of childbearing and rearing. It's time to relinquish the past and go on with the present and future—to make sure our marriage is on the road to fulfillment.

We're at a stage where we realize that we have more control over our destiny. We can say no or yes to life as it pleases us. Our experience and well-honed talents should be fully utilized, not left to rust. They contribute richness to our marriage.

Consider the words of Jim Conway:

A couple should make sure their future plans include full utilization of all the gifts, strengths, and abilities of both of them. If the woman is underchallenged, doing routine, mundane, piddling things that are unimportant to her, she will have a shrinking self-image, less marriage satisfaction, and difficulty moving through the late-forties stress period.[7]

That goes for the fifties and sixties too. Both Jim and his wife Sally preach and practice that wisdom. Not only are they both authors, but both are engaged in an exciting ministry which includes an organization they started called Christian Living Resources through which they minister to families around the world who are in the mid-life stage.

Men, the most attractive women are those who radiate a love of people and a love of life along with self-confidence and an air of accomplishment. The development of their inner resources leaves them with more to give.

You women, whether married or single, should take the initiative. You are responsible for your own growth, for what happens to you the rest of your life. Remember Mavis, the middle-aged woman who climbed out of the ruts into a fulfilling career. Develop your full potential with education and training. And while you're at it, give yourself lots of credit for your experience, which may be worth more than formal education. The resulting self-confidence brings a sparkle to your personality, and a feeling of self-worth.

Alice and I do many things together. But we have found that shared interests do not preclude respect for individuality and privacy. We accept the fact of our individual, God-given uniqueness. Each of us is endowed with certain capabilities, interests, rights, and needs. We recognize that each person needs some time alone and time with other people apart from our "coupleness."

No, we do not expect ourselves or our circumstances to ever be perfect. But our relationship is much closer to a Beethoven symphony than it is to a Spike Jones cacophony.

CHAPTER THIRTEEN

A BLUEPRINT FOR SELECTING WHERE TO LIVE

Occasionally over the past few months Lois and David had been talking about retirement, but they had not gotten around to talking about where to live. Lois assumed David would respect her desire to stay in their present home. Then suddenly one day, from behind the magazine he was reading, David casually announced that he knew a great place to retire 1500 miles from Lois's beloved home.

Her mind churned. David had struck a blow against domestic tranquility. After considering her options—divorce, murder, or running the car over his golf clubs—Lois reverted to female practicality—negotiation. Bargaining chips, that's what she needed. "I'll tell you where I hid your fishing gear if. . . . You can buy that sport car you've always wanted if. . . . I'll cook your favorite foods instead of my diet meals if. . . ."

There are things more earthshaking than choosing your retirement location and home. But not many. A husband doesn't always realize how a woman identifies with her home. Many times it becomes as much a part of her as a child. Of course, the strength of the attachment varies greatly among women, and sometimes the husband has stronger feelings about his home than his wife. But the point is that the husband and wife often feel very differently about a change.

To state the obvious, when people retire some move and some don't. But there are actually two parts to the domicile decision: where to live and what kind of dwelling to live in.

Sometimes mistakes happen when these decisions are made without careful consideration. Some mistakes can be reversed, but often bridges are burned that are difficult or impossible to rebuild.

Your domicile decision is an important building block of your lifestyle. It has a decided effect on your feelings about retirement. A very complex thing, it involves quality of life, climate, work or hobby preferences, living costs, cultural opportunities, and health care availability. And then there are those things which have psychological and spiritual overtones such as churches, self-esteem, friends, and proximity of children.

My intent is not to make your decision for you but to weave a tapestry, a picture of others' experiences. Woven into the tapestry are the threads of mistakes as well as the threads of success (the wise things people have done when making this crucial decision). Perhaps by looking at these examples you will be able to form a clear vision of what you want.

HOW TO CHOOSE YOUR SLICE OF PARADISE

Fantasies are fun. But don't paint too many dream pictures before you share them with your spouse who may be painting a different scene.

You may dream about playing tennis in the January sun of Arizona while your spouse harbors a vision of a sailboat anchored in a snug and picturesque port in Maine.

Some people thrive in new settings. Some can't be dragged

from their present home with a twenty-mule team. While the lure of a faraway place and a fresh start is appealing, be cautious. Putting down new roots requires a lot of effort and considerable risk at a stage in your life when you might rather spend your energy on rest and relaxation on your own turf.

With careful planning, you can fulfill your fantasies and also satisfy your practical requirements. Possibilities for your retirement paradise fall into four broad categories:

▶ Relocating in a foreign country
▶ Relocating in another state
▶ Relocating in the same state, new area
▶ Staying where you are

But then there is the decision as to whether to mix with the general population, join an enclave of mostly retirees, or live in a senior citizens' village. I have not discussed the senior citizens' village in detail because only a small minority of retirees make that their first choice. However, the factors of location and type of dwelling that I do discuss are just as important in that situation as when living among the general population. Some people decide to join an enclave or live in a senior citizens' village after years of retirement living elsewhere. No matter when such a decision is made, it is important to evaluate and compare the different villages.

So much for the rough framework within which to make your decision. The chart in figure 13.1 will help you organize your thinking using the common criteria mentioned above; delete those which aren't important to you and add others which are.

Select two or more tentative locations represented in the chart by the columns labeled A, B, C, and D. You may want to consider more or less than the four the form calls for.

In the left-hand column are the attributes for which you will evaluate and compare the tentative locations. After each attribute in this column is a number that represents what you feel is the relative importance of that attribute compared to all the others in the column. These numbers range from 1 to 3, 3 being the most important and 1 the least. According to the arbitrary numbers I chose to illustrate, health care is an important 3 while cultural opportunities are a less important 1. But, of course, these are just for example. You should choose your own numbers. And of course, it might be wise for you and your spouse to fill out separate forms. That helps to understand each other's feelings and provides endless opportunities for communication.

These "relative importance" or weight numbers become the first number in the equation in column A.

Now you are ready to rate the different locations. I suggest a number rating system, 0 for very poor, 1 for poor, 2 for fair, 3 for good, and 4 for excellent. The higher the number, the better you like that particular attribute of that location. If, for example, location A is Phoenix, Arizona, and you choose a 4 for a particular attribute, you are saying that Phoenix is attractive from that standpoint. Note that if living costs were very high in a location, they are undesirable and you would choose a 1 for that attribute. These rating numbers become the middle number in the equations in column A.

Now you multiply the numbers in the attribute column by the rating numbers and arrive at the right-hand number in the column A equation. Adding these right-hand numbers together gives you the total at the bottom of the column A. The same procedure is used for each location you wish to evaluate. The highest number at the bottom of the columns A, B, etc. gives you your overall best choice.

If you don't like the results, then you should reconsider some of your ratings or assigned weights. You may find that you have 2 or 3 overriding considerations, so you want to skip the others and go directly to "move." But I suggest you not be too hasty. If you go through this exercise, you may discover real feelings that will surprise you.

Attributes	Location			
	A	B	C	D
Quality of life, 2	2 × 3 = 6			
Climate, 3	3 × 4 = 12			
Work opportunities, 2	2 × 1 = 2			
Good place for hobbies/sports, 1	1 × 4 = 4			
Living costs, 3	3 × 2 = 6			
Cultural opportunities, 1	1 × 2 = 2			
Health care, 3	3 × 1 = 3			
Friends, 1	1 × 2 = 2			
Proximity of children, 2	2 × 2 = 4			
Churches, 2	2 × 3 = 6			
Totals	47			

Figure 13.1.   An exercise for evaluating potential retirement locations.

This evaluation system looks easy on paper, but that's something of an illusion. The obstacle you must hurdle is the assignment of rating numbers for the various locations. You can talk to people who have been there, read dozens of magazine articles, but other people's opinions are no substitute for seeing it and feeling it yourself. A vacation or two in a place will help, but living in a place for a full year may change the tint of your rose-colored glasses. A five-day trip to the mountains for skiing is one thing, but shoveling snow and wading through slush for four months out of the year is entirely different.

This goes for other attributes besides climate. For example, breaking into the local social circles—making friends—can be very tricky, sometimes impossible.

To gain perspective on this little problem, review figure 13.1

again. How many people would agree on the relative importance (weight) or the ratings you have assigned? Agreement on all of them would be as rare as a pink penguin. And remember that what an accountant would consider a first-class work opportunity would not excite a mechanic.

One way to check out your uncertainty about the attributes of various locations is to lease your present home, move to an area you think you would like, and rent for a year. This greatly improves your odds of making a good evaluation. But it probably means waiting till you retire to make your domicile decision, which is usually better anyway because then you have a much more accurate picture of your total situation. No need to hurry. Your special paradise will still be there next year.

HOW OTHERS HAVE CHOSEN A LOCATION

Most retirees stay put. Their philosophy, "Why give up what I like for an unknown?" makes a lot of sense to people who are contented with their location. Other people dream a new scene, and in living their dream, they have some varied and interesting experiences. As you will see, some of the following scenes have yet to be fully played-out on the stage of life.

» Charles and Vivian «

Charles is a sailing enthusiast who loves salmon fishing. His wife, Vivian, says, "The sailing I like; but when he goes fishing, I'll probably stay home to paint and read."

They lived in Los Angeles. Several years before he retired, Charles, an aerospace engineer, talked Vivian into spending a vacation in the Puget Sound area of Washington state. They fell in love with it and spent several more vacations there and explored the western half of the state on long drives.

They found a roomy house on two gorgeous acres overlooking Hood's canal, an arm of Puget Sound. The undisturbed natural landscape and fantastic view enchanted them, and the price tag of 25 percent less than their present house had them drooling.

They bought it. Three years later, Charles retired and they sold their Los Angeles house.

Their three children were grown and had, years before, scattered to the four winds. Charles and Vivian severed all other connections and moved to their "promised land."

I asked Charles why they had bought such a big house. While he was thinking about the question, Vivian answered it. "I like lots of space and with no one else around to mess it up, it is easy to take care of. Besides," she winked, "I need lots of room for the pictures I'm going to paint. There's an unfinished room over the garage that I'm fixing up for a studio, and the big deck is an outdoor studio in good weather."

Then Charles chimed in, "And I have my own office in the fourth bedroom and my shop in the garage." He is doing part-time consulting for an aerospace company, which leaves plenty of time for sailing and fishing.

They both concede that the change of climate took getting used to. But their activities are varied enough so they always have something interesting to do regardless of the weather. After three years, they are as happy as two mosquitoes in a blood bank.

» Albert and Bonnie «

On the premise that, "This place is getting too crowded for us," Albert and Bonnie began their building project six years before Albert planned to retire. They sweated through four years of spare time "do-it-yourself." Then just before they installed the finishing touches, Albert's company made him an early retirement offer he couldn't refuse.

Their slice of paradise is a beautiful three-acre "ranch" at the 4500-foot altitude in the Sierra Nevada Mountains. A year-around stream flows across one corner, and pines and cedars fringe their building site. Enthusiastic hikers and skiers, they are ensconced on the edge of their dream.

Money was not a problem. They leased their home in the city (it was almost paid for) when they moved to the mountains. As Bonnie put it, "We reserved a foothold in the valley. When we get too decrepit to strap on our skis, we may become 'flat-landers' again. In the meantime this is great."

» Dennis and Caroline «

Dennis had made a bundle in commercial real estate and decided to retire at age sixty. Both he and his wife, Caroline, were in good health, and Dennis knew that, with all his energy, he would need a challenge to keep happy. He had a great idea for a new business which could be pursued in the Midwest where he and Caroline were raised. Remembering their happy youth in the small town, they decided to leave Oregon and return to the old scene.

Neglecting to investigate, Dennis and Caroline were sand-bagged by their assumptions. After all, they had visited the home town ten years ago, and it seemed to be suspended in time. Little had changed since they lived there. The delightful weather that May was matched by the friendliness of the people.

They sold their home and moved. Back in the small midwestern community, they built a big, beautiful home. But before their home was finished, the surprises began.

Many of their old friends had moved away. Dennis and Caroline were painting their dream on a new canvas. For various reasons, they were not accepted by the local populace. Their efforts to make friends and to break into the social circles were rebuffed.

Rejected. The sky was falling. Dennis' new business did not go well. Caroline felt like she was a prisoner in her own home. All of which made the climate seem more rugged than they remembered it. After three years, they threw in the towel. Defeated and disillusioned, they sold their house and returned to Oregon.

This is not a criticism of the people of that town. They may have had very good reasons for acting the way they did. The point is that Dennis and Caroline could have saved themselves time, pain, and money if they had investigated before they pulled up their roots. If they had rented a house for a year, they would have gotten a feel for the place, discovered the problems, and then could have pulled out with less muss and fuss.

TACTICS FOR SELECTING YOUR CASTLE

Few retirees will give up their creature comforts for a little grass shack, no matter what the location. Nearly all people choose something from the following list because each of these dwellings can be comfortable depending on what your standards are and what you are willing to pay for it.

- ▶ Motor home/trailer/yacht
- ▶ Mobile home
- ▶ Condominium/town house
- ▶ Apartment
- ▶ Conventional single family house

Another consideration is whether to buy or rent. One approach to a selection is to view your retirement as a "moving" picture: one type of dwelling now and something else later. For example, you may choose to travel around for a year in a motor home, live in a conventional home for the next several years, and later move into a condominium in a senior citizens' village.

Again, you can organize your thoughts with a chart if you believe that more than one type of dwelling might be acceptable. (See figure 13.2. You may want to add other attributes.)

SOME PEOPLE'S CASTLES

I pointed out earlier that others' opinions have limited value when it comes to selecting a place to spend your later years. The same holds true for choosing a type of dwelling. I'm talking here

| | Type of Home | | | |
Attributes	A	B	C	D
Appropriate for chosen location				
Satisfies self-image				
Space for hobbies, storage, etc.				
Fits the budget				
Good neighbors				
Facilities for entertaining				
Space for overnight guests				
Choice of friends				
A good home base				
Totals				

Figure 13.2.   Evaluating various types of homes.

about opinions based on hearsay, travel folder hype, the high pressure of real estate salesmen, and short-term vacation experiences. But the long-term, true-life experiences of other people will stimulate your thinking. In figure 13.2, by type of home, I mean motor home, mobile home, single family house, condominium, etc.

Select your own weighting and rating system and assign the numbers, according to your own judgment, like you did in figure 13.1. I have shown only four columns for four different types of homes, feeling that you probably won't consider more than that. Now you are ready to fill in the spaces in figure 13.2 and compare the different types of homes. It can be very helpful to talk to several people who have lived, or are living, in the different types of homes. But in the final analysis you must decide what suits you, not what is satisfactory for someone else.

In most cases, when you hear what happened to them as a result of their decisions, you will be able to imagine how you would have felt and acted in the same circumstances. You can learn from their mistakes, as well their wise decisions, and you can reach your retirement paradise without frustrating side trips.

» Frank and Karen «

To live their dream, Frank and Karen bought a big motor home. They sold their condominium in a metropolitan area, pulled up their roots, and hit the road. Joining a club of other motor-home owners, they basked in the winter sunshine of the southwest and enjoyed cool summers on the Pacific coast.

They did not mourn friends left behind. They made the rounds of their three children in different states. But on their third visit in six months, they noticed a certain coolness.

They saw places they had always wanted to see and played golf two or three times a week. They met a lot of interesting people who were always on their good behavior. That part was okay. But since people were always movin' on, friendships were very casual and without any depth. A week here and two weeks there, it was two years of almost constant travel.

One rainy morning, Frank and Karen were having their second cup of coffee and staring out of the window at the side of their neighbor's motor home. Karen got up to take the hot rolls out of the warming oven.

Frank wrapped one hand around his hot coffee cup, stroked his day-old beard and said, "I sure do enjoy a cup of coffee on a rainy day like this." Then he shifted his conversational gears, "But, you know, I'm getting bored with travel."

That remark pushed Karen's button. She laid the steaming rolls on the table as her words tumbled out. "I've been doing some thinking, too. This is a beautiful motor home, but I'm ready for a change. I miss some things more than I thought I would. I need more space. These walls are closing in on me. I like travel, but I want a permanent home to go back to. And our good old friends, I miss them. What do you suppose Judy and George are doing now? We haven't heard from them for a long time."

Because of increased prices, Frank and Karen could not afford to buy a home in the area they had left. But they found a solid, old house in a small town two hours from their previous location. Although they still do some traveling, they are much happier having a larger and permanent home to come back to. They are making some good friends there and occasionally are visiting some of their old friends.

Hindsight is 20-20. Frank and Karen agree that they should have kept their condominium and rented it out while they were traveling around in their motor home. That way they would have had more options when they decided to make a change.

» Mort and Ethel «

Their conventional, frame home in a good location was completely paid for, and Mort and Ethel knew it was worth at least twice the going price of a mobile home. Why not sell, buy a mobile, and invest the difference?

When Ethel retired a year before Mort, she began looking at mobile-home parks and comparing the prices of the houses, space rentals, and maintenance fees. She discussed mobile homes with friends, but their enthusiasm did not entirely dispel her doubts. True, there were positive reasons for living in a mobile home in a nice park—almost no yard work; a recreation center with swimming pool, meeting rooms, recreation room, and other amenities. Friendly active seniors organized parties and bridge groups, and they looked out for each other.

But Mort and Ethel also learned of some of the negatives about this kind of domicile. In most cases the owners of the dwellings do not own the land on which they are parked. They are only renting space. Except for special laws or ordinances, the owner of the land can sell to a developer for another use, such as commercial building, and all the residents will have to move. There are exceptions. I know of one park where the residents, with the cooperation of the owner, formed a corporation and bought him out. Each resident owns stock in the corporation and has a voice in the operation of the park. And more important, they are secure from being forced to move.

Most mobile homes appreciate in value very slowly or not at all as compared to other houses. They are quite expensive to move if you want to go to another location. Your alternative is to sell, but they are often harder to sell than a conventional home.

Mort and Ethel weighed the pros and cons and felt that the pros outweighed the cons. But still being uncertain, they worked out a good scheme. They had enough money for a down payment on the mobile home. By renting their present house for a year, they had enough income to make the payments on the mobile home. By keeping their present house and living in the mobile home for a year, they could return to their old house if the move turned out to be a mistake. This scheme provided peace of mind.

At the end of a year, the mobile home won. Mort and Ethel sold their old house and invested the extra money in conservative bonds for additional spendable income. Of course, they could have kept the old house as an investment, but they didn't want the hassle of managing rental property.

» Elmer and Charlene «

When Charlene first showed Elmer the ads, he dismissed them as so much rotten cotton. "Eliminate the work and worry. Be free to enjoy life as it was intended to be lived. Buy a condominium or town house in our development and live happily ever after." The ad boasted of security systems and the most modern of construction, not to mention recreation facilities, swimming pool, and so many other amenities it made your head swim.

After about six months of thinking and many plumbing repairs later, Elmer conceded without Charlene having to use subliminal suggestion. Very methodical, he listed the pros and cons.

He disliked gardening because it took time away from other things he would rather do. Competing with insects, pulling weeds, mowing lawns, were not his idea of a reason for living. He was no match for gophers and moles that had Ph.D.s in Dirty Tricks.

And then there was the state of their house to be considered. Plumbing, roof, paint, furnace, and carpeting all needed repair or replacement.

Elmer and Charlene decided that with the children gone, they didn't need their big house. Elmer's main requirement was a large garage that he could use for his shop. Three bedrooms were adequate with one a guest room and the third a sewing room. If they could find a town house with just the right design and amenities in a nearby location, they would move.

And that's exactly what they did.

THE LAST WORD ON LESSONS LEARNED

Selecting your castle and its location is the one retirement decision I recommend making after you retire. You needn't hurry. Your special paradise will be waiting for you when you're ready for it. And if you presently own a home, keep it until you're sure of what you want to do. Remember the first law of successful retirement? Do all of the groundwork while you're still working. Make a preliminary comparison of options and when you can spend a year personally investigating your tentative choice, you're ready to make a final decision. The reason is simple. You need lots of time to do it right.

A word of caution. The true stories I related above were merely intended to stimulate your thinking. I'm not suggesting that you do what someone else has done. It may be right for them but not for you. Sometimes couples have followed each other like lemmings and drowned in a sea of regret. Have your own good reasons for what you do.

CHAPTER FOURTEEN

ABUNDANT LIVING IN OUR LATER YEARS

Erik, age fifty-six, had just emerged from his own private hell. He had undergone cancer surgery to remove a football-sized tumor, followed by chemotherapy. After months of physical and mental torture, his doctor gave him the good news: "No more evidence of cancer."

As we talked, his mood became philosophical, and he said, "That experience changed my perspective. I now have a new time frame, BC—before cancer, and AC—after cancer.

"For years I put off thinking seriously about what's important—just reacting to what seemed most urgent at the time. Then, wham! My mind whirled like an out-of-control, double timing, movie projector. I saw myself falling off the cliff like the stagecoach in one of those old cowboy movies. Suddenly deciding what's important became both the most important and the most urgent matter in my life.

"But, you know, that's not the end of it. It's now almost two years since that first shock of cancer and time seems to be distorting my vision of what's important. I remember a cheap pair of field glasses I used to have. I could get them in focus but the least little jolt would throw them out of focus. Just like that, the urgent is now sneaking in again and distorting my vision of what's important. I still have a lot to learn about values."

GROWING IN SELF-UNDERSTANDING

Those little maps they place at the entrances to big shopping centers are priceless. I can always manage to find my destination because they tell me where I am. Without that, I could wander around for days and maybe starve to death.

Although goals facilitate human growth, we also need an awareness of where we're starting from. We need to understand ourselves in order to see a route to our destination. We can attain wholeness and fulfillment in direct proportion to our self-understanding. But there is another powerful force that directly affects our growth, and that is our relationships with other people and with God.

A good book to assist you in your quest for self-understanding is one written by Dr. Cecil Osborne. Down to earth, authentic, and speaking to real people about real issues, this book is titled *The Art of Understanding Yourself.*

In the foreword, Dr. William Parker asserts that Osborne is a realist who expresses a rare combination of religious insight and psychological truth which, when applied, can be helpful to the reader where he is.

He goes on, "This book is an invitation to insight, to growth, to identity, to re-affiliation. It deserves to be read by all who are in search of a better way of life within, so they may relate meaningfully to their fellowmen. It is an invitation to move toward wholeness, by understanding how one is divided against oneself. It is therefore an invitation to life."[1]

As we travel through life we tend to get weighed down with excess baggage, like the junk that mysteriously accumulates in the garage and that we resist discarding because we think someday it may be useful. We can travel light and enjoy it if we dump some of the heavy negatives and just latch on to the affirmatives.

We can discard the idea that we have to please everyone, and just relax and enjoy being ourselves. The older we get, the less we feel a need to prove anything. We can discard the "plague of shoulds." (You should do this; you should do that. You should act or feel this way or that.) Who says so? Just because one person thinks a certain way doesn't mean you should. We're not all cut out with the same cookie cutter.

Then there are the prejudices and biases that we once felt enhanced our security. These back-breaking weights are no more useful than dead flashlight batteries.

Here is a list of some of the excess luggage that we can discard or, better yet, trade in on something positive:

▶ taking ourselves too seriously
▶ making apologies for being eccentric
▶ using pointed and unkind humor
▶ worry/anxiety
▶ envy
▶ false guilt
▶ fears
▶ regrets

There are many other pieces of junk that may hide in our baggage without our being aware of it. But if we find any, a ruthless purge will lighten our load. Now we will have room for the positives, and it is amazing how much easier they are to carry. Finally, we need to love ourselves, warts and all, and grow on from there.

AVOIDING THE INTROSPECTION TRAP

It's important to stay in communication with your insides—to be alive to your feelings and needs without being narcissistic about it. But excessive introspection can trap you.

There comes a time in life when examining yourself too closely is like looking at your face in a convex mirror. Every pore looks like a moon crater and every wrinkle like the Grand Canyon. You can get so wrapped up in yourself that it's like living in a straight-jacket. Before that happens you need to look outward and get involved with other people.

Some of the happiest people are those whose hobby is people. Not only do we need people to maintain our sense of values and perspective, but we need them because we need to be needed by them.

Paradoxically, our relationships may be close and warm, and yet, we can enjoy a certain detachment from others that increases our insightfulness. In other words, we can stand back from the trees and get a better view of the forest. We can accept people for what they actually are, not for what we wish they were. We can love our fellow human beings with no strings attached.

We can be honest but flavor the honesty with love and compassion.

And that's part of what is meant by integrity—honesty with compassion; soundness and wholeness, yet individuality; high moral and ethical standards; a willingness to help other people wherever and whenever we can.

THE FUTURE GROWS FROM THE PRESENT

My wife is one of the kindest most diplomatic persons I know. But Alice knows that, with me, diplomacy doesn't always get through. She has her own way of bringing me back to earth from my flights of fancy and excursions into the future.

We were talking the other day, and I told her I was trying to think of something profound to wind up this chapter. Out of the blue she said, "Does the here and now you've been writing about include trash bags? The trash bag under the sink is full and needs emptying."

Well garble my floppy! I had just been returned to the here

and now. Alice had reached right into my word processor and converted the profound to the practical.

Dumb habits are often acquired early in life. I can't even remember when I began postponing satisfaction and fulfillment in the mistaken belief that the future was all that mattered. The opposite extreme that has become rather common is the demand for instant gratification. I think both extremes generate their own problems.

But back to my dumb habit which, incidentally, I have been working hard to modify. This habit manifests itself in empty-headed declarations such as:

▶ Just wait till I solve this problem. Then I can do what I really want to do.

▶ Just wait till I get my raise. Then we'll be able to take that vacation.

▶ Just wait till the company cuts out the overtime. Then I will take the family to the beach.

▶ Just wait till I retire. Then I'll be happy.

What am I trying to say? This book is about planning for your future—for your retirement. Yet I appear to be attacking the concept of thinking about the future. Clarification is in order.

It's like driving a car. You can drive a car and carry on a conversation at the same time. Your driving is directed to your destination, a place you will reach in the future. You may be following a map (plan) to get there. But at the same time you are enjoying the here-and-now conversation with your passengers.

So it is with retirement preparation. While you're stirring up the dust with high-powered planning, assessing the possibilities, and following the plans with action, you can carry on vital living by embracing the second law of successful retirement, which is:

The best preparation for the next stage of life is to wrap the present stage in positive attitudes and live this stage to the fullest.

Filling the present with good living (it may even include cheer-fully carrying out the trash) is the best way to build a foundation for the future. It is saying yes to life: childhood, youth, adult-hood, maturity, old age; but not getting stuck on one tape. There is sweet music on the next tape, and the next, and the next. When you know that, it's easier to lay aside the last one.

OUR INNER JOURNEY

This book is about a journey: how to get from where you are to where you want to be when you fold up your present career. How to assure happiness and fulfillment in your later years by what you do and how you live in your earlier years. Like any big change in life, retirement is as much an inner journey as an outer change. And therein lie the beauty and the possibilities.

But just because we have a beautiful flight plan and have made a perfect take-off doesn't mean we won't encounter bad weather along the route. We will be challenged by problems and obstacles; frustrations are as much a part of life as are the tri-umphs. Retirement doesn't change that.

There are times in any stage of life when living seems like a process of three steps forward and two steps back. But when we cut through the facade of an impossible situation, we often find it is a great opportunity in disguise. What happens to us is not the most important factor. How we respond to what happens (devel-oping the habit of looking for the opportunities in a situation) becomes an integral element of life quality.

We have been bombarded with both spoken and written words about quality of life mostly having to do with outside environ-mental conditions such as air and water quality. I do not discount their importance. Nor do I discount the importance of finances. But all it takes is some mature, rational thinking to realize that of even more importance to our quality of life is our personal and inner environment: mental, spiritual, and physical health.

It is my experience that the majority of people who are happy in their later years are those who, for many years, have had an abiding faith in God. They know that God loves and cares about them. They have established a relationship with God.

Faith, hope, and love are synergistic. Each tends to produce the others. They harmonize and generally coexist. They feed and support each other. And when they all exist "inside your skin," you will have the healthy glow of true happiness.

To have a life filled with loving relationships is to really live. The rewards for learning the true meaning of love are immense. The most eloquent paean to love is that written by the apostle Paul in 1 Corinthians 13 where he says in part that love is:

> patient and kind
> not jealous or boastful
> not arrogant or rude
> not always insistent on its own way
> not irritable or resentful
> forgiving
> trusting
> full of hope
> unending

Finally he closes that triumphant hymn with that famous line. "And now these three remain: faith, hope and love. But the greatest of these is love" (1Cor. 13:13).

SECRETS OF ABUNDANT LIVING

After surviving a Nazi concentration camp, psychiatrist Viktor Frankl wrote:

> There is much wisdom in the words of Nietzsche "He who has a why to live for can bear almost any how." I can see in these

words a motto that holds true for any psychotherapy. In the Nazi concentration camps, one could have witnessed (and this was later confirmed by American psychiatrists both in Japan and Korea) that those who knew that there was a task waiting for them to fulfill were most apt to survive.[2]

During our early and middle years of adulthood, our primary purpose may be to care for a spouse and children. It may be an ambition to achieve, to help one's fellow humans. Or it may be a desire for wealth. Whatever our reasons for living at one stage, they may disappear or change in priority at a later stage. At every age, we need a reason for living—a task, a purpose that gives us a genuine sense of usefulness.

But I think that abundant living is far more than a task.

What is the secret of those people who reach retirement happy, continue happy, and become more and more alive as they grow older? Here is my distillation of the more meaningful secrets.

▸ They have put their lives and attitudes in order before they ever reach their vintage years.

▸ They have planned well for the future, while living fully in the present.

▸ Their sense of values has kept them awake to what's really important. They are selective, doing only those things which they consider worthwhile and which their time and talents allow them to do well.

▸ They have a capacity for love and warm relationships with other people.

▸ They do not try to fashion the rest of the world in their own image, nor do they allow others to program them.

▸ They define self-worth in terms of vitality and psychological and spiritual values rather than social status, financial position, or professional achievement.

▸ They feel a strong connection to a community of friends.

▶ They don't take themselves too seriously. They feel no need to continually prove themselves.

▶ They say yes to life, willing to enthusiastically try new things.

▶ Through faith, hope, and love, they have a sense of meaning in their lives.

▶ They have the peace of mind that comes from a right relationship with their Creator.

It is my hope that this book will enrich your life. That you will dream, plan, and then live abundantly. This is the first day of the rest of your life. If you live your later years in security, confidence, and fulfillment, it will be because you learn how now and choose to continue growing.

NOTES

Chapter 1. POISED ON THE EDGE OF ADVENTURE

1. Tony Lamb and Dave Duffy, *The Retirement Threat* (Los Angeles: J. P. Thatcher, Inc., 1977).
2. Richard Eisenberg, "Planning Now for Your Successful Retirement," *Money Guide—Planning Now for Your Successful Retirement*, 1985, 6.
3. Paul Tournier, *Learn to Grow Old* (London: SCM Press Ltd., 1972), 13.
4. Ibid., 13.

Chapter 2. THE REAL WORLD OF MONEY MATTERS

1. Investment Forum, Minneapolis, MI, 1985.
2. Richard Eisenberg, "Planning Now for Your Successful Retirement," *Money Guide—Planning Now for Your Successful Retirement*, 1985, 6.
3. Thomas E. Ricks, "People's Perception of the Elderly As Being Poor Is Starting to Fade," *Wall Street Journal*, 19 December 1985, Western edition, Sec. 2.
4. Clare Ansberry, "Aging Program," *Wall Street Journal*, 26 December 1985, Western edition, p.1.
5. Gregory Stricharchuk, "Fading Benefit," *Wall Street Journal*, 26 August 1987, Western edition, p.1.
6. Richard Eisenberg, "Figuring Out What You'll Need," *Money Guide—Planning Now for Your Successful Retirement*, 1985, 16.
7. John R. Connell, LaVerne L. Dotson, W. Thomas Porter, Robert E. Zobel, *Touche Ross Guide to Personal Financial Management* (Englewood Cliffs, NJ: Prentice-Hall, Inc., 1985).

8. Statistical Abstract of the United States, (U. S. Department of Commerce, Bureau of the Census, 1986), 68, 69.

Chapter 3.   PERSONAL FINANCIAL PLANNING

1. Frank I. Reilly, *Investments* (Chicago: The Dryden Press, 1982).

Chapter 4.   TRAINING FOR THE VINTAGE YEARS

1. Brendon Gill, *Lindbergh Alone* (New York: Harcourt Brace Jovanovich, 1977).
2. Howard Shank, *Managing Retirement* (Chicago: Contemporary Books, 1985), 252.
3. Paul Tournier, *Learn to Grow Old* (London: SCM Press Ltd., 1972), 18, 19.

Chapter 5.   ENERGIZED WITH WINNING ATTITUDES

1. Viktor Frankl, *The Doctor and the Soul: From Psychotherapy to Logotherapy* (New York: Bantam Books, 1952).
2. David D. Burns, *Feeling Good: The New Mood Therapy* (Bergenfield, NJ: Signet Book, New American Library, 1980), 29.
3. Harry W. Hepner, *Retirement—A Time to Live Anew* (New York: McGraw Hill, 1969), viii.
4. Arthur Bloch, *Murphy's Law* (Los Angeles: Price/Stern/Sloan, 1979).
5. Burns, 11.
6. Ibid., 12.
7. Charles R. Swindoll, *Strengthening Your Grip* (Waco, TX: Word Books, 1982), 207.
8. Morton Hunt, "Beat Your Bad Moods for Good," *Reader's Digest,* June 1986, 17.
9. Frank B. Minirth and Paul D. Meier, *Happiness Is a Choice* (Grand Rapids, MI: Baker, 1978).

Chapter 6.   BUILDING A NEW IDENTITY

1. Allan Fromme, *Life After Work* (Published by AARP, 1984), 15, 16.
2. Howard Shank, *Managing Retirement* (Chicago: Contemporary Books, 1985), 12.

Chapter 7. PLANNING THE REST OF YOUR LIFE

1. Charles R. Swindoll, *Strengthening Your Grip* (Waco, TX: Word Books, 1982), 18.
2. Maxwell Maltz, *Psycho-Cybernetics* (Hollywood: Wilshire Book Co., 1965).
3. Joyce Brothers, *How to Get Whatever You Want Out of Life* (New York: Ballantine Books, 1978), 25.
4. Ibid., 32–33.
5. Ibid., 35.

Chapter 8. STRATEGY FOR GROWING IN NEW DIRECTIONS

1. Gail Sheehy, *Passages* (New York: E. P. Dutton, 1976), 353.
2. M. Scott Peck, *The Road Less Traveled* (New York: Simon and Schuster, 1978).

Chapter 9. SMOOTHING THE ROAD WITH ROBUST HEALTH

1. Maggie Scarf, "Images That Heal," *Psychology Today,* September 1980, 32.
2. Bruce Larson, *There's a Lot More to Health Than Not Being Sick* (Waco, TX: Word Books, 1981), 140.
3. Ibid., 141.
4. *The American Medical Association Family Medical Guide,* 1982.
5. Werner Graendorf, *A Happy Look at Aging* (San Bernardino: Here's Life Publishers, 1985), 53–66.
6. Stuart Berger, *How to Be Your Own Nutritionist* (New York: William Morrow, 1987).
7. Stuart Berger, "Should You Take Vitamins?" *Parade Magazine,* 22 Feb. 1987.
8. Berger, *How to Be Your Own Nutritionist.*
9. Graendorf, 35, 36.
10. Ibid., 36

Chapter 10. FLAVOR LIFE WITH QUALITY LEISURE

1. Paul Tournier, *The Adventure of Living* (New York: Harper and Row, 1965).
2. Tim Hansel, *When I Relax I Feel Guilty* (Elgin, IL: David C. Cook, 1979), 29.

Chapter 11. KEEPING YOUR MARRIAGE ALIVE

1. Allan Fromme, *Life After Work* (Washington, D.C.: American Association of Retired Persons, 1984), 55.
2. Special Survey titled "The Private Life of the American Woman," *Ladies Home Journal,* April 1987, 98.

Chapter 12. STRATEGY FOR A VIBRANT MARRIAGE

1. David and Vera Mace, *We Can Have Better Marriages If We Really Want Them* (New York: Abingdon Press, 1974).
2. Fr. Chuck Gallagher, *The Marriage Encounter* (Garden City, NY: Doubleday, 1975), 36.
3. Mace, 121.
4. M. Scott Peck, *The Road Less Traveled* (New York: Simon and Schuster, 1978), 81.
5. Ibid., 98.
6. Ibid.
7. Jim Conway, *Men in Mid-Life Crisis* (Elgin, IL: David C. Cook, 1978), 170.

Chapter 14. ABUNDANT LIVING IN OUR LATER YEARS

1. Cecil G. Osborne, *The Art of Understanding Yourself* (Grand Rapids, MI: Zondervan, 1967), Foreword.
2. Viktor E. Frankl, *Man's Search for Meaning* (Boston: Beacon Press, 1963), 164, 165.

BIBLIOGRAPHY

Berger, Stuart. *How to Be Your Own Nutritionist.* New York: William Morrow, 1987.

Blanton, Dr. Smiley. *Now or Never (The Promise of the Middle Years).* Carmel, NY: Guideposts Associates, 1959.

Brothers, Dr. Joyce. *What Every Woman Should Know about Love and Marriage.* New York: Ballantine, 1985.

Burns, Dr. David D. *Feeling Good (The New Mood Therapy).* New York: Signet, 1980.

Chew, Peter. *The Inner World of the Middle Aged Man.* New York: Macmillan, 1976.

Conway, Jim. *Men in Mid-Life Crisis.* Elgin, IL: David C. Cook, 1978.

Conway, Sally. *You and Your Husband's Mid-Life Crisis.* Elgin, IL: David C. Cook, 1980.

Dayton, Edward, and Ted Engstrom. *Strategy for Living.* Glendale, CA: Regal Books, 1976.

Dobson, Dr. James. *What Wives Wish Their Husbands Knew about Women.* Wheaton, IL: Tyndale, 1975.

Dobson, Dr. James. *Emotions: Can You Trust Them?* Ventura, CA: Regal, 1984.

Dobson, Dr. James. *Straight Talk to Men and Their Wives.* Waco, TX: Word Books, 1984.

Engstrom, Ted W. *The Pursuit of Excellence.* Grand Rapids, MI: Zondervan, 1982.

Frankl, Viktor E. *Man's Search for Meaning.* New York: Simon and Schuster, 1959.

Frankl, Viktor E. *The Doctor and the Soul.* New York: Bantam Books, 1952.

Gardner, Joseph. *Eat Better, Live Better.* New York: Reader's Digest, 1982.

Geist, Harold, *Psychological Aspects of Retirement.* Austin, TX: Thomas, 1968.

Gold, M. *The Older American's Guide to Housing and Living Arrangements.* New York: Consumers Union, 1984.

Green, G. *How to Start and Manage Your Own Business.* New York: McGraw-Hill, 1975.

Hallman, G. Victor and Jerry S. Rosenbloom. *Personal Financial Planning.* New York: McGraw-Hill, 1982.

Hansel, Tim. *When I Relax I Feel Guilty.* Elgin, IL: David C. Cook, 1979.

Hardy, C. *Your Guide to Financially Secure Retirement.* New York: Norton, 1984.

Hayes, Helen. *Our Best Years.* New York: Doubleday, 1984.

Krammer, J. J. *The Mobile Home Guide.* New York: Bobbs-Merrill Co., 1982.

Levinson, Daniel. *Seasons of a Man's Life.* New York: Knopf, 1978.

Mace, David and Vera Mace. *We Can Have Better Marriages If We Really Want Them.* New York: Norton, 1984.

Maltz, Dr. Maxwell. *Psycho-Cybernetics.* Hollywood, CA: Wilshire Book Co., 1965.

Mehr, Robert I. *Fundamentals of Insurance.* Homewood, IL: Richard D. Irwin, Inc., 1983.

Morgan, Marabel. *The Total Woman.* Old Tappan, NJ: Revell, 1973.

Osborne, Cecil G. *The Art of Understanding Yourself.* Grand Rapids, MI: Zondervan, 1967.

Peck, M. Scott. *The Road Less Traveled.* New York: Simon and Schuster, 1978.

Peterson, Jean R. *Organize Your Personal Finances.* Whitehall, VA: Betterway Publications, 1984.

Porter, Sylvia. *Sylvia Porter's Your Own Money.* New York: Avon, 1983.

Porter, Sylvia. *Sylvia Porter's New Money Book for the 80s.* New York: Avon, 1980.

Pryor, Hubert. *Your Retirement Housing Guide.* Long Beach, CA: American Association of Retired Persons (AARP), 1975.

Quinn, Jane Bryant. *Everyone's Money Book.* New York: DeLacorte, 1979.

Reilly, Frank I. *Investments.* Chicago: The Dryden Press, 1982.

Schaie, K. Warner and James Geiwitz. *Adult Development and Aging.*

Boston: Little, Brown and Company, 1982.

Shedd, Charlie. *Letters to Karen: On Keeping Love in Marriage.* New York: Avon, 1968.

Shedd, Charlie. *Letters to Philip.* Old Tappan, NJ: Revell, 1969.

Sheehy, Gail. *Passages.* New York: E. P. Dutton, 1976.

Schuller, Dr. Robert H. *You Can Become the Person You Want to Be.* New York: Hawthorn Books, 1973.

Schuller, Dr. Robert H. *The Be-Happy Attitudes.* Waco, TX: Word Books, 1985.

Schuller, Dr. Robert H. *Be Happy—You Are Loved.* Nashville, TN: Thomas Nelson, 1986.

Schuller, Dr. Robert H. *The Peak to Peek Principle.* Garden City, NY: Doubleday, 1980.

Sloane, L. *The New York Times Book of Personal Finance.* New York: New York Times, 1985.

Swindoll, Charles R. *Living on the Ragged Edge.* Waco, TX: Word Books, 1985.

Swindoll, Charles R. *Living Above the Level of Mediocrity.* Waco, TX: Word Books, 1987.

Swindoll, Charles R. *Growing Strong in the Seasons of Life.* Portland, OR: Multnomah, 1983.

Swindoll, Charles R. *Strengthening Your Grip.* Waco, TX: Word Books, 1982.

Tournier, Dr. Paul. *To Understand Each Other.* New York: Jove Publications, 1967.

Weinstock, Harold. *Planning an Estate.* New York: McGraw-Hill, 1982.

Wright, H. Norman. *Communication: Key to Your Marriage.* Ventura, CA: Regal Books, 1974.